Personal Readers

for Emergent and Beginning Readers

Donald Bear,
Carol Caserta-Henry,
and Darl Venner

Published by
Teaching Resource Center

Published by
Teaching Resource Center
P.O. Box 82777
San Diego, CA 92138

Illustration: Linda Starr
Editor: Laura Woodard

Printed in the United States of America
ISBN: 1-56785-067-7

Donald Bear is director of the E. L. Cord Foundation Center for Learning and Literacy and is involved in outreach Reading Buddies tutoring programs, in which he works with children who experience difficulties learning to read and write. Donald is a professor in the Educational Specialties Department at the University of Nevada, Reno. He has been a third- and fourth-grade classroom teacher, and currently conducts research in literacy development across languages and among English language learners. Donald is one of the co-authors of Words Their Way and the companion video and supplements.

Carol Caserta-Henry, M. Ed., has used Personal Readers in tutoring programs and classrooms for the past sixteen years. She has worked as a classroom teacher, a reading teacher, and a literacy consultant with teachers throughout Northern Nevada and the United States. She has developed several workshops to assist teachers in the implementation of tutoring programs and effective literacy practices, and is co-author of The Reading Buddies Manual. She has worked with the authors of Words Their Way in developing materials, and has presented at Words Your Way conferences. Carol earned her Master's Degree from the University of Nevada, Reno. She lives in Reno with her husband, Ken, and their two daughters, Jenni and Abbey.

Darl Venner, M. Ed., is a primary classroom teacher who is a doctoral candidate in Literacy Studies at the University of Nevada, Reno. She has taught special education and grades one through three. She earned her Master's Degree from the University of Nevada, Reno, and has been a presenter at Words Your Way conferences for the past five years. Darl has been dedicated to effectively helping children acquire literacy skills and sharing her knowledge with others. She has used Personal Readers in tutoring programs and classrooms for nine years. Ms. Venner is a native Nevadan and resides in Reno.

Dedication

To the teachers who have used Personal Readers to help students succeed as readers.
Donald, Carol and Darl

Acknowledgements

Thanks to Dr. Shane Templeton for his mentoring and friendship
D.R.B., C.C.H., D.A.V.

Thanks to my family, whose encouragement and love make all things possible, and to the fantastic teachers, tutors, and students I have had the honor to work with over the years. Your input and delight with Personal Readers have made this book come alive!
C.C.H.

Thanks to my mom, Patricia Venner, for always cheering me on and believing in me, and to my friends, who have stood by me. This book wouldn't have been possible without the wonderful and caring staff from Marvin Moss Elementary School!
D.A.V.

CONTENTS

Section I: What You Need to Know About Personal Readers

Introduction 3
- What Are Personal Readers? 3
- How To Use This Book 3
- How Students Use Personal Readers 3
- How Personal Readers Fit into Your Current Reading Program 4
- Why Do We Use Personal Readers with Emergent and Beginning Readers? 4

Key Practices for Creating and Using Personal Readers 5
- Language Experiences: Group Experience Charts and Individual Dictations 5
  - Creating Group Experience Charts (GECs) 5
  - A 7-Day Group Experience Chart Cycle 6
  - GEC Points to Remember 7
  - Individual Dictations 7
  - Ideas for Language Experiences 8
- Rhymes in the Personal Reader 9
  - Format for Using Rhymes 9
- Readers Theatre 10
  - Format for Using Readers Theatre 10

Using Personal Readers with Emergent Readers 10
- Characteristics of the Emergent Reader 10
- Group Experience Charts 11
- One-Sentence Dictations 11
- Rhymes 12

Using Personal Readers with Beginning Readers 13
- Characteristics of the Beginning Reader 13
- Group Experience Charts 13
  - Support for Early Beginning Readers 13
  - Support for Middle Beginning Readers 14
  - Support for Middle to Late Beginning Readers 14
- One-Paragraph Individual Dictations 15
- Rhymes 15

Readers Theatre in Personal Readers 16
- Word Study in Personal Readers 16
  - Sound Boards 16
  - Word Banks and Beginning Readers 16
  - Word Bank Activities 17-18

Organization of the Personal Reader 19-20

The Process of Repeated Readings 20

References 21

Section 2: Personal Reader Activities with Emergent and Beginning Readers

Activity 1: Pineapple Explorations . . . 25
Activity 2: Bubble Explorations . . . 39
Activity 3: Color Explorations . . . 54
Activity 4: Pipe Cleaner Fish . . . 67
Activity 5: Rock Explorations . . . 80
Activity 6: Flower Explorations . . . 94
Activity 7: Chicken Soup with Rice . . . 108
Activity 8: Magnet Explorations . . . 120
Activity 9: Worm Races . . . 133

Appendix

Parent Note – Emergent Readers . . . 146
Parent Note – Beginning Readers . . . 147
Parent Note in Spanish – Emergent Readers . . . 148
Parent Note in Spanish – Beginning Readers . . . 149
Look What ___ Is Reading . . . 150
Personal Reader Reading List . . . 151
Alphabet Graph . . . 152
Letters I Know! . . . 153
Alphabet Award . . . 154
Beginning Consonants, Short and Long Vowels Sound Boards . . . 155
Blends and Digraphs Sound Boards . . . 156
Word Bank Word Chips . . . 157
Word Bank Words . . . 158
Word Bank Graph: Way to Go! . . . 159
Word Bank Award . . . 160
Word Bank Baseball . . . 161
Bingo Boards . . . 164
Boom! Cards . . . 165

SECTION 1

What You Need to Know About Personal Readers

Introduction

What Are Personal Readers?

Personal Readers are collections of familiar materials stored in thin folders for students to reread. Students reread selections in their Personal Readers to acquire concept of word, engage in word study, and increase their sight vocabularies, fluency, expression, and comprehension. Personal Readers are an ideal way to collect familiar materials for support reading.

How To Use This Book

This section describes in depth the primary practices for creating and using Personal Readers. This includes a discussion of how to use the Personal Readers with students learning to speak and read in English as a second language. This discussion of fundamentals is followed by nine Personal Reader lessons with the supporting blackline masters to create Personal Readers for students in the Emergent and Beginning stages of literacy development. These lessons include the rhymes, directions for student dictations, and word study activities that accompany the lessons.

How Students Use Personal Readers

The Personal Readers contain copies of familiar materials such as group experience charts, rhymes, poems, individual dictations, and passages from leveled books distributed for use by publishers. These materials should be printed in a 16- to 24-point font. Small leveled books can be slipped into the pockets of Personal Readers.

Students read and reread the materials in their Personal Readers with your support until they can read the materials independently. Students turn to their Personal Readers during free reading time to reread materials they are confident that they can reread accurately. Personal Readers are adapted for transition activities with English language learners. Through repeated reading of these familiar materials, students see themselves as readers, and their success motivates them to read more. Students enjoy taking their Personal Readers home to show others what they are able to read.

Students in the same stage of development have very similar materials in their Personal Readers. The materials provided in the nine lessons are organized to show what materials to use with Emergent and Beginning readers.

How Personal Readers Fit into Your Current Reading Program

Teachers incorporate Personal Readers into existing reading and spelling programs. The Readers can be used in a variety of reading and word study activities:

Reading Activities

- Familiar rereading
- Repeated reading
- Timed reading for fluency and accuracy
- Readers' Theatre
- Sustained Silent Reading

Spelling/Vocabulary Activities

- Harvesting words for word banks
- Collecting interesting words
- Word hunts for spelling patterns or related words
- Looking for words to add to word collections (e.g., "action words" or "words to use instead of said")

Why Do We Use Personal Readers with Emergent and Beginning Readers?

Students are proud of their Personal Readers and you'll find them useful in your teaching for the following reasons:

- **Authorship:** Students have an inherent interest in reading their own words.
- **Reading fluency:** Memory and the familiar language patterns promote fluency for Beginning readers.
- **Concept of Word:** By writing down their actual words, students see their speech converted to print. Pointing to the words when rereading helps students solidify their concept of word.
- **Content Area Support:** When students dictate about a subject they have been studying in class they strengthen their understanding of the subject.
- **Sharing Opportunities:** Students reread their dictations to each other and their families. Students feel good about sharing their literacy.
- **Collecting Words for Word Study:** After rereading their dictations, students collect words and acquire a stable sight vocabulary. These known words are used in word study activities.

Key Practices for Creating and Using Personal Readers

Emergent and Beginning readers learn about word boundaries and concept of word when they reread familiar materials. Rereading familiar materials is a common practice that has been a mainstay of literacy instruction through the ages (Huey, 1976), going back to ancient times when students learning to read sacred texts would track in writing the prayers they had learned to recite orally.

Language experience reading activities use students' personal experiences and language to create the material that they will reread. The first part of this section focuses on key practices underlying language experience activities.

Rhymes are also ideal for Emergent and early Beginning readers to reread, as rhymes are memorable and enjoyable for the wonderful sounds, rhythms and ideas they contain. This section offers ideas for using rhymes in small group instruction.

Language Experiences: Group Experience Charts and Individual Dictations

A directed introduction to literacy is possible in what are called language experience activities. In this process, you show students the processes of reading and writing as you guide them through an experience, discuss the experience, complete a written account of the experience, and then reread the account, altogether as a group.

It's important to be explicit as you demonstrate, with students' involvement, how to take ideas and language and create writing that they'll reread. In this demonstration process students learn that "what we can talk about we can write down, and what we write down we can read" (Stauffer, 1970). This, the Language Experience Approach, is the basis for much of this book.

Creating Group Experience Charts (GECs)

Group experience activities are wonderful opportunities for students to see their speech converted into print. These activities begin with students sharing some sort of concrete experience such as sampling foods, mixing colors, or interacting with animals. During the experience, encourage a rich discussion. As a result, students will have more language at their disposal when dictating their sentences for the chart.

Collect sentences about the experience from students and write them on a chart. With Emergent readers, guide the group in creating one simple sentence. With Beginning readers, collect one sentence from each student. Once the writing is complete, read and reread the chart to and with students, pointing to the words as you go. Also type these charts on individual pages and place them in students' Personal Readers. Over the next week, students can frequently reread and work with words from the chart.

A 7-Day Group Experience Chart Cycle

Day 1

- Gather a small instructional group.
- Have a group experience and encourage discussion throughout.
- Record an exact sentence from each student in a chart.
- Reread the chart to the group.
- Let students make any additions or changes.
- Have the group decide on a title.
- Read and point to the words while students watch.
- Choral read while a student points to the words.
- Have students point to words as they read their own sentences.
- Reread the whole chart.
- Type the chart and make copies for Day 2.

Day 2

- Put individual copies of the chart in the students' Personal Readers.
- Reread the chart to the group.
- Choral read while one or two students point to the words.
- Have the students point to and reread either their sentence or the whole chart.
- Have partners read the student copies in the Personal Readers.
- Have each student underline three or four known words on the chart.
- Have the students write these words at the bottom of the page.
- Have the students read in partners.
- Have the students draw a picture or find a photo to go with the experience.

Days 3-7

- Reread the selection together.
- Point randomly to underlined words on individual copies.
- Have students write underlined words on small, 2" x 3" rectangles of paper or card stock ("word chips") for word banks.
- Send home Personal Readers for rereading.
- Continue with extension activities.

GEC Points to Remember

For the Discussion:

- As the discussion starts to wind down, move the stimulus for the experience (e.g., food cooked, rocks collected) out of sight or put it on display by the chart. The stimulus can distract students if it is left in their hands.
- Encourage students to share a sentence that adds a new idea to the chart.
- If you use overheads instead of chart paper, you can face the students while you're writing on the overhead projector.
- Read the chart with fluency and expression so that students can copy your model when they reread. Be careful not to reread too rapidly or too expressively.
- Allow students to read the dictation to at least two different partners in the group to improve fluency and reading rate.
- Use Wikki Stix or highlighter tape to call attention to interesting words on the chart. Focus on features related to your students' development. For example, Emergent and early Beginning readers could look for words that begin with the /s/ sound.

For Student Work:

- Make sure that students have enough room on the typed page to draw a picture. This picture will remind them of the content of the story.
- Enlarge the text to 24- to 28-point size on the individual copies.
- Make at least three copies per student of the chart: one for the Personal Reader, one to take home, and one to cut apart.
- Encourage students to put a tally mark at the bottom of the page each time they reread the chart in their Personal Readers.
- Write word bank words on 1" x 2" word chips for students.
- Have students reread the GECs in their Personal Readers to parents, siblings, stuffed animals, and pets, and record themselves reading.

Individual Dictations

Collect individual dictations in much the same way as GECs. For purposes of rereading, keep dictations by Emergent readers to one sentence. As students become more adept at tracking print, collect one-paragraph dictations. From middle Beginning readers collect one-paragraph dictations. Late Beginning readers' dictations may be two or three paragraphs. The crucial factor to keep in mind is the students' ability to reread the dictation. Text that is too long or unfocused may be difficult for students to read. As you will see in the examples on page 11, dictations may be recorded in two languages to support the transitions of English language learners.

Ideas for Language Experiences

A classroom is like a living museum full of as much activity and focused attention as students can give. The activities below are just a few ideas for experiences that can lead to GECs and individual dictations. The starred (*) activities are covered in detail in this book.

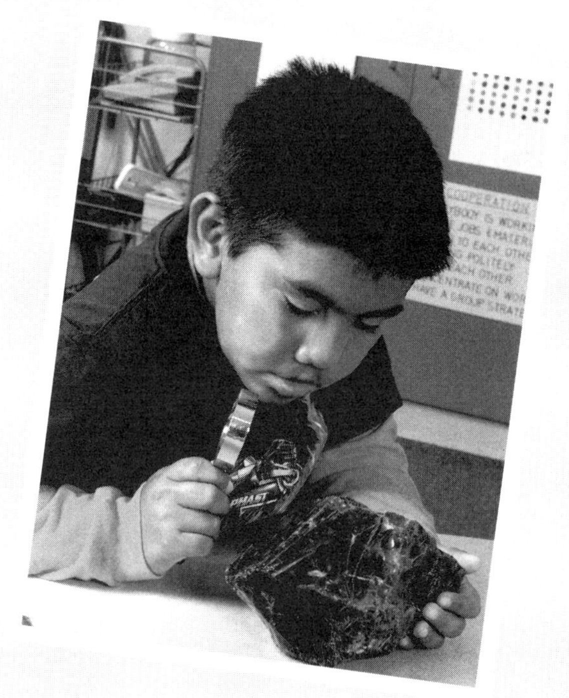

Foods to Make or Taste

seeds for counting
spices
gum or candy
smoothies
soup *
pineapple *
various fruits
pumpkins
various potato chips
pancakes
popcorn
ice cream
international foods
cookies
different types of water
pickles
sweet and sour (compare/contrast)

Activities for Discussion

stage worm races *
take nature walks
do science experiments
make pipe cleaner fish *
listen to favorite music or play instruments
go on field trips
share family photographs
dissect flowers *
work with clay or salt-flour dough
respond to picture books or a video
create a flannel board story
share collections
examine rocks *
examine and cut up gourds
explore with magnets *
mix colors *
blow bubbles*

Animals to Observe

birds
bunnies
cats
chinchillas
crickets
dogs
fish
frogs
gerbils
hamsters
hedgehogs
hermit crabs
lizards
snakes
spiders
turtles
worms

Rhymes in the Personal Reader

Students enjoy the rhythm and repetition of simple nursery rhymes, jump rope jingles, and songs. Rhymes and chants are easy to use and easy to find in books and on the Internet. Many of the songs by children's folk singers are good for Emergent and Beginning readers to reread. When you write these rhymes on a chart and on individual papers, students can then practice reading and rereading them. Memory and rhyme support these early attempts at matching speech to print.

Selecting rhymes of the appropriate length and complexity is an important consideration. When Emergent and early Beginning readers come to reread 2- to 4-line rhymes, slow down the pace of the recitation of the rhyme, and remove some of the rhythm in your voice so students can concentrate on matching what they see with what they say. When you teach the rhyme you may want to add hand and body movements. Emergent and early Beginning readers like this movement; this activity allows us to repeat the rhyme more often for memorization.

Students who are middle Beginning readers can come off the page if they are reading rhymes that are only two lines long. For this reason, middle and late Beginning readers read rhymes that are quite a bit longer, anywhere from two to four stanzas.

Format for Using Rhymes

Day 1

- Teach the rhyme to your students orally. Do not use the printed words at first.
- Chant the rhyme until it has been memorized.
- Add a finger play or dramatize the rhyme.

Day 2

- Write the rhyme on chart paper in large print.
- Read the rhyme to the group while pointing to each word.
- Choral read while pointing to each word.
- Choral read while a student points.
- Type copies of the rhyme in large print.
- Place the copies in the Personal Readers for repeated practice and for later use in word hunts.

On following days:

- Reread the rhyme together in various ways.
- Have students read the rhyme while "reading the room."
- Have students use Wikki Stix or highlighter tape to highlight known letters or words.

Readers' Theatre

Readers' Theatre provides students with simple text to practice and then perform. Props are very simple and costumes are not usually involved. It is not necessary for students to memorize their lines because they hold their scripts while performing. You can make books into Readers' Theatre scripts or create your own scripts. Readers' Theatre scripts are provided for many of the activities in this book.

Format for Using Readers' Theatre

Day 1

- Give the script to the students in your small group.
- Read the script to the students.
- Choral read the script.
- Have students read the script in partners.

Day 2

- Assign students to the parts.
- Have the students practice reading the script with their partner or group.
- Have the students focus on reading with fluency and expression.
- Choral read while a student points to the words.

Day 3

- Have the students practice performing their script.
- Have the students perform for their class.
- Have the students perform for other classes (if so desired).

Personal Readers with Emergent Readers

Emergent readers are young children who are experimenting with print and oral language. They engage in pretend reading and writing and eventually make the connection between key sounds and single letters as a way to represent words. Emergent readers are typically found in kindergarten and first grade classrooms. The characteristics below will help teachers identify students who are Emergent readers.

Characteristics of the Emergent Reader

- Scribbles letters and numbers ("symbol soup")
- Lacks concept of word
- Has minimal letter-sound correspondence
- Represents words with key sounds and single letters ("k" for "cat")
- Engages in pretend reading and writing
- Enjoys memorizing rhymes and ditties

Group Experience Charts

Students share and discuss an experience, and their comments about the experience are recorded on the Group Experience Chart, or GEC. For Emergent readers, collect one simple sentence from each student in the group. It is important to keep the text short, simple, and structured to help students track and reread. Once the writing is completed, read the chart to and with the students, pointing to the words as you read. Over the next week, students frequently reread the sentence.

Here is a sample of a simple text.

Story # ____ Date ______

Fish are fun.

One-Sentence Dictations

When you want to work with one child at a time, you can take a one-sentence dictation from the Emergent reader. Collect these one-sentence dictations in much the same way as you would complete a group experience chart, except with a single student.

Here are steps to follow for collecting a one-sentence dictation:

- Have each student dictate a sentence that can be typed and put in his or her Personal Reader.
- Leave extra space between each word and type it in a 24- to 26-point font.
- Have the student draw a picture to help remember the content of the sentence. This can be a good seatwork or homework activity.

For English language learners, writing the sentence in both languages provides additional support.

Story # ____ Date ______

I like fish.

A mí me gustan los peces.

Rhymes

Students enjoy the rhythm and repetition of simple nursery rhymes. When using rhymes with Emergent readers, teach the rhyme orally first. When the students have memorized the rhyme, write a couple of the lines on a chart; a whole rhyme would include too much text for Emergent readers to track. Students can then practice reading and rereading the rhymes, which supports the development of concept of word.

Here is a rhyme to chant with students and sample pictures to use.

10 Little Fishes

1 little, 2 little

3 little fishes.

4 little, 5 little

6 little fishes.

7 little, 8 little

9 little fishes.

10 little fishes swimming in a row.

10 Little Fishes

1 little,

2 little

3 little fishes.

Here are a few lines from the poem as we might write them on the chart.

Follow the format on page 9 for rereading and using the rhyme.

PERSONAL READERS WITH BEGINNING READERS

Beginning readers have started to learn words and are learning to read simple texts. They use invented spelling in their writing and use initial and final consonants to represent words. Beginning readers make the connection between key sounds and single letters as a way to represent words. They are typically in first and second grade. The characteristics below will help you identify students who are Beginning readers.

Characteristics of the Beginning Reader

- Spells initial and final consonants
- Begins to add a vowel in the middle of words
- Has rudimentary/functional concept of word
- Finger-points while reading word by word
- Memorizes text
- Reads the pictures

Group Experience Charts

Students share and discuss an experience, creating a Group Experience Chart in the process. For Beginning readers, collect a sentence from each student in the group. Once the writing is completed, read the chart to and with the students, pointing to the words as they are read. Over the next week, students frequently reread and work with words from the chart.

Support for Early Beginning Readers

- Begin each sentence with the student's name.
- Color-code each sentence.
- Keep the text simple and mostly patterned.

Here is an example of text that would appear on a Group Experience Chart:

Story # _____ Date ______

Hedgehogs

Annahy said, "It feels prickly!"
Susan said, "It feels like stickers."
Lia said, "It feels hard."

Student draws a picture here.

Support for Middle Beginning Readers

- Write student names at the end of the sentences.
- The sentences don't have to follow a pattern.

Story # ______ Date _______

Hedgehogs

"I pricked my finger!" said Annahy.

"His hair felt like stickers," said Susan.

"Hedgehogs feel hard!" said Lia.

Student draws a picture here.

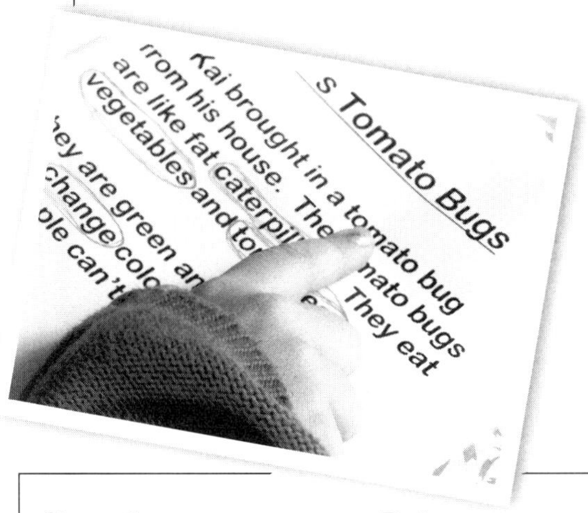

Support for Middle to Late Beginning Readers

- Eventually, eliminate the extra support of their names or the color coding.
- When they seem ready, start writing the sentences in paragraph form as shown in the example to the right.

Story # _____ Date _______

Hedgehogs

Hedgehogs feel prickly! They can also feel hard. They have pointy things that feel like stickers. We like having a hedgehog in our room.

Student draws a picture here.

One-Paragraph Individual Dictations

As students become more adept at tracking print and no longer need the support of their names or color coding, you can start using a paragraph format. The information is collected from one student rather than the whole group.

Story #_____ Date_____

Fishing With Dad

I went fishing with my dad. We went to the river and got on a big rock. We had to be quiet. Dad helped me. I held the fish pole for a long time. I didn't catch any fish!

Student draws a picture here.

Twinkle, Twinkle

Twinkle, Twinkle, little star
How I wonder what you are.

Up above the world so high
Like a diamond in the sky.

Twinkle, Twinkle, little star
How I wonder what you are.

Rhymes

Students enjoy the rhythm and repetition of simple nursery rhymes. When using rhymes with Beginning readers, teach the rhyme orally first. When the students have memorized the rhyme, then you can write it on a chart. After writing the rhyme in large print on chart paper, follow the format listed on p. 9 for rereading and using the rhyme. Rereading the rhymes supports the development of concept of word.

Here is a rhyme to teach your students.

Readers' Theatre in Personal Readers

Students who are middle or late Beginning readers enjoy Readers' Theatre activities in which they take turns reading their parts with one or two partners. Keep the activity limited to a few students, or else have students share parts.

There are easy Readers' Theatre pieces in the activities that follow. Support students as they read the "plays" and then monitor their rereading to be sure their pace is not too rapid, and that other students follow along as they read.

Word Study in Personal Readers

Sound Boards

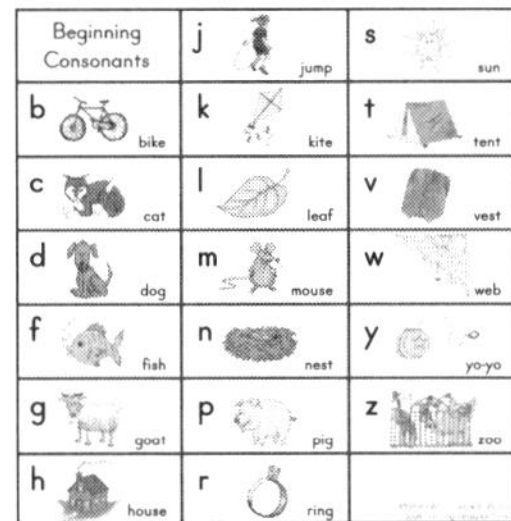

Sound boards are charts of pictures and letters that help students remember Beginning consonant sounds, blends and digraphs, as well as short and long vowels. They are described in detail in *Words Their Way* (Bear, Invernizzi, Templeton, Johnston, 2004). Reproducible copies can be found in Part III here.

Copy the sound boards and place them in Personal Readers or tape them to desks so students can refer to them when reading and writing. Use the *Beginning Consonants Sound Board* for Emergent readers. As students progress, add the *Blends and Digraph Sound Boards,* the *Short Vowel Sound Boards,* and finally, the *Long Vowel Sound Boards.*

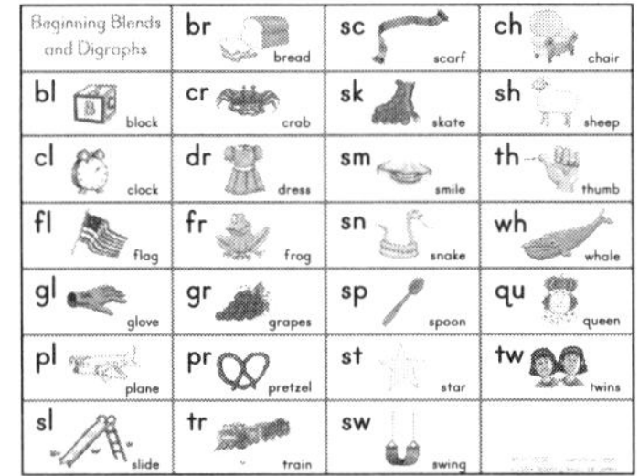

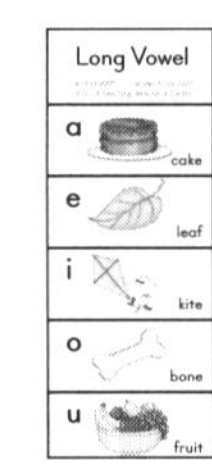

Word Banks and Beginning Readers

Word banks are collections of words selected by students that they remember well enough to know in isolation (Stauffer, 1980). The words are written on small cards or word chips and gathered over time.

What types of words do students place in their word banks? We often find sight words such as *the* and *went* or interesting words like *dinosaur* and *Christmas.* Students review the words in their word banks regularly as a way to support the growth of their sight word vocabularies and their understanding of letter-sound correspondence.

Personal Readers are an excellent place for students to collect words for word banks. In the back of the Personal Readers we place a baggie that contains recently collected word bank words. These words are reviewed daily, and words that are not read accurately after a few days are discarded. This way, when students use their Word Bank words for other activities such as sorting and playing games, they are working from known words and can then focus on the patterns being studied.

Collecting Words for the Word Bank: The words in students'word banks are known words that are used in word study activities. Observe students reading their word bank words at least once a week. Teach students to place unknown words to the side if they cannot read the word in a few seconds. Model this for them over a few days. In her classroom, author and literacy specialist Shari Nielsen develops a "class word bank" where discarded words are stored for later review. We also like to use a word bank form on which students record the words and the dates as they add them to their growing word banks. Occasionally, we have students read the words on these lists as another way to check their sight vocabularies.

Recommended Guidelines

- Students underline three or four known words in each rhyme or chart.
- With your help, students write the words at the bottom of the page on which they are found.
- Write these words on word chips for each student.
- Students write their initials and the number from the chart on the back of each word chip.
- Using their copies of the text, students can refer back to the context of the story to help remember the word, if necessary.
- Students keep word chips in zip-lock baggies in the back of the Personal Reader.
- As students collect more words, they move the most familiar words from the baggie into the larger word bank, which they keep in a little box or tub.
- Students use the words in the baggie and the tub for word work.

Word Bank Activities

Word Hunts

The students use the stories and rhymes in their Personal Readers to hunt for words that follow a pattern being studied such as:

- Beginning and ending consonants
- Rhyming words
- Phonograms (word families)
- Blends and digraphs
- Short vowel CVC words

These words can be recorded on charts in the room.

Word Sorting

The students sort the word bank words into categories. Some possibilities include:

- *Concept sorts:* sort words into columns by categories such as: animals/not animals; colors/not colors; or living/not living.
- *Sound sorts:* sort for words that begin with a certain sound, words that rhyme, words that have the same ending sound, or same short vowel sound.
- *Open sorts:* sort the words and have another student guess how the words were sorted.

Alphabet Strips and Word Banks
Place a large alphabet strip on the floor and have the students sort word bank words by the beginning sound and place them under the correct letter on the strip.

Three Guesses
The students take turns providing clues about a selected word, such as "It rhymes with..." or "It begins the same as...".

Word Bank Baseball
This game helps students review their word bank words. Home runs are made by correctly reading the words. See Section 3 for directions and a game board.

My Pile/Your Pile
This game helps students improve fluency and accuracy when reading word bank words. Students quickly read through their words, keeping the ones read correctly. Students try to increase the number of correct words each time they play.

Boom!
Inside a can are four cards that say *Boom!* The students also place their words in the can, and the cards are mixed together. Students take turns pulling out the words and reading them. Unknown words are placed behind the can. When one of the students pulls a *Boom!* card, the game stops and students count their words. The winner is the one with the most words. The game starts over after each *Boom!* card is pulled. See Section 3 for blacklines.

Pick-Up
A student places twelve word bank words face-up on the table. One partner reads a word and the other partner has to pick up the correct word card. Then they reverse roles. This can be made more challenging by choosing words beginning with the same letter, such as *bat, ball,* and *big.* Variations:

- Pick up a word that begins with a certain letter or sound.
- Pick up words that all contain a certain letter anywhere within the word.
- Pick up words that rhyme with ___.
- Pick up words that start like ___.

Bingo
Each student gets a photocopy of the bingo board blackline from Part III and a handful of bingo chips. Each student selects sixteen words from the word bank and writes one in each box. Someone shuffles the word cards and places them face down. The caller draws a card and reads it. Any player who has that word on his card covers it with a chip. The first person to have four in a row is the winner.

Making Sentences
Once students have thirty sight words collected, they can create sentences from their word cards with your help, if necessary.

Concentration
Using a duplicate set of cards for 10-15 word bank words, students can play a game of concentration or memory in a group or in partners.

Organization of the Personal Reader

How do Personal Readers fit into classroom routines? Many teachers keep the Personal Readers in buckets or boxes stored in a central place: by the door for students to pick up when they come in, near where reading groups meet, or right in their desks for convenience. Set aside time at least twice a day for students to read three or four of the latest entries in their Personal Readers. Once every five to seven days, have them add a new piece to the Personal Readers. This means that students will stop rereading one of the older or less memorable selections and replace it with the new one. We have developed a variety of forms to help you communicate with parents and follow students' progress in using the Readers. In addition to the blackline masters for the activities, the following forms are provided in Part III:

Parent Notes about Personal Readers

These notes to parents explain the purpose of the Personal Readers and what they and other family members can do to support their child's literacy growth. This includes letters for both Emergent and Beginning Personal Readers. Spanish versions are also included.

Personal Reader Reading List

Parents sign this form after listening to their child read the story or dictation. You might choose to fill in which stories the students should read.

Look What _____ Is Reading

Once the student's name is filled in the blank, this form is used to keep track of the books the Beginning reader has read.

Letter Identification

This chart is used to keep track of the upper and lower case letters that a student knows. This generally is for late Emergent readers and early Beginning readers.

Letter Award

This is an award given to a student when he or she has learned both upper and lower case letters.

Word Bank List

All words found in the word bank are recorded on this list. You or a tutoring buddy should be the one to write the words to ensure that correct spelling is used.

Word Bank Graph

Students tally the number of words in their word banks on this graph in an effort to reach one hundred.

Word Bank Award

This is the award given to students when they have collected and can read one hundred words in their word banks.

Word Bank Baseball

Use the direction page and game sheet for playing Word Bank Baseball with word bank words.

Bingo Boards

This page is used as a template to play Word Bank Bingo.

Boom! Cards

These cards can be cut and used to play Boom! with word bank words.

Sound Boards

The following Sound Boards are included:

- Beginning Consonants Sound Board: for Emergent and early Beginning readers to help them match letters and sounds
- Blends and Digraphs Sound Board: for Beginning readers who are learning blends and digraphs
- Short Vowel Sound Board: for middle Beginning readers who are starting to put vowels in words when writing
- Long Vowel Sound Board: for late Beginning readers who begin to explore long vowel sounds

The Process of Repeated Readings

The group experience stories and content dictations from the Personal Reader are used to support reading fluency. Rereading these helps students develop both accuracy and fluency.

Develop a schedule for rereading dictations. Rereading can be practiced with some independence. Contract with the student to reread recent dictations three times a day. (The Personal Reader Reading List found in Section 3 can be used to keep track of who the student reads to.)

Work toward accuracy and fluency in rereading. For a late Beginning reader, 90-100 words per minute is a good reading rate to achieve after several rereadings. Often, assigning student reading partners provides welcome assistance with monitoring reading rates. You might want to tape record yourself reading the student's dictation so that he or she can follow along. The student listens to the tape and then practices reading without the tape. When students think they can read the text as well as you, they should let you know and then read for you.

Reread related texts. Once students acquire a good reading rate and accuracy with the dictations, they can reread the text on which the dictation was based. A student might need the support of the teacher or a reading buddy for this. You may also provide related texts that are written at the reader's independent level to include in the student's Personal Reader.

Other ways to support reading accuracy and fluency

- Find texts for students to read that are at their instructional level.
- Have students practice poetry and Readers' Theatre and then present these to other students or classes.
- Have a "poetry fest" and let students partner up to present a poem to the class.
- Have students read together in paired reading, echo reading, choral reading, and reading with books on tape.
- Model fluent reading in Teacher Read-Alouds.

References

Bear, D., Barone D., Pruyn, M., & Schneider, R. (1998). *Developing literacy: an integrated approach to assessment and instruction.* New York: Houghton Mifflin.

Bear, D., Invernizzi, M., Templeton, S., & Johnston, F. (2004). *Words their way.* New Jersey: Pearson Prentice Hall.

Caserta-Henry, C., Bear, D., & Del Porto, C. (1997). *Reading buddies manual: teaching in a schoolwide literacy program the developmental way* Center for Learning and Literacy, MS 288, University of Nevada, Reno, Nevada 89557.

Carle, Eric (1987). *The very hungry caterpillar.* New York: Scholastic.

Cowley, Joy (1990) *The jigaree.* Washington: Wright Group.

Dixon, C. & Nessel, D. (1983). *Language experience approach to reading (and writing).* Hayward, CA: Alemany Press

Fry, B. E., Kress, J. E., and Fountoukidis, D. L. (2000). *The reading teacher's book of lists* (4th ed.). Jossey-Bass.

Hall, M. (1980). *Teaching reading as a language experience.* Columbus, OH: Merrill.

Johnston, F. R., Invernizzi, M., and Juel, C. (1998). *Book buddies: guidelines for volunteer tutors of Emergent and Beginning readers.* New York: Guilford Press.

Kress, J. E. (2002). *The ESL teacher's book of lists.* John Wiley & Sons.

Martin, Bill Jr. (1983). *Brown bear, brown bear, what do you see?* New York: Holt & Co.

Morris, D. (1999). *The Howard Street tutoring manual.* New York: Guilford Press.

Nelson, O. & Linek, W. (1999). *Practical classroom applications of language experience.* Boston: Allyn and Bacon.

Nessel, D. & Jones, M. (1981). *The language experience approach to reading.* New York: Teachers College Press.

Stauffer, R. G. (1980). *The language experience approach to the teaching of reading* (2nd ed.). New York: Harper and Row.

Templeton, S. (1997). *Teaching the integrated language arts* (2nd ed.). Boston: Houghton Mifflin.

Walsh, (Stoll) E. (1995). *Mouse paint.* San Diego, CA: Harcourt.

Young, S. (1994). *Scholastic rhyming dictionary.* New York: Scholastic.

SECTION 2

Personal Reader Activities
With Emergent and Beginning Readers

There are nine complete Personal Reader activities in this section. The suggested format for each activity is basically the same, involving seven days of activities with the developmental groups in your classroom.

Structure of Personal Reader Activities

Materials:	List of materials needed for the activity
Day 1:	The Language Experience Chart the Experience
Day 2:	Rereading in the Personal Reader
Days 3-7:	Extension Activities

Directions for each activity are organized by developmental levels for Emergent, Beginning and late Beginning readers. Additional blackline masters are provided in Section 3.

Blacklines in the Personal Reader Activities

Additional blacklines for extending the Personal Reader experience are provided in Section 3, starting on page 145.

Activity 1: Pineapple Explorations 25
Pineapples rhyme 30
Pineapples rhyme by lines 31
Upper- and lowercase matching letters for "pineapple" 32
"A Pineapple Poem" 33
"A Pineapple Poem" by lines 34
Pineapple pattern book pages 36
Readers Theatre: "Here Is a Pineapple" 37
Pictures of large and small pineapples 38

Activity 2: Bubble Explorations 39
Bubbles rhyme 44
Bubbles rhyme by lines 45
Upper- and lowercase matching letters for "bubbles" 46
"Bubbles, Bubbles" poem 47
"Bubbles, Bubbles" by lines 48
Readers Theatre: "Bubbles" 50
Bubbles flip book pages 51
Pictures of large and small bubbles 53

Activity 3: Color Explorations 54
Colors rhyme 59
Colors rhyme by lines 60
Upper- and lowercase matching letters for "colors" 61
"Catch a Rainbow" poem 62
"Catch a Rainbow" by lines 63
Colors pattern book pages 64
Readers Theatre: "Magic in the Sky" 65
Mouse outlines for mixing colors 66

Activity 4: Pipe Cleaner Fish 67
Fish rhyme 72
Fish rhyme by lines 73
Upper- and lowercase matching letters for "fishy" 74
"I'm a Tiny Fishy" poem 75
"I'm a Tiny Fishy" by lines 76
Fish pattern book pages 77
Readers Theatre: "Fishing with my Daddy" 78
Pictures of large and small fish 79

Activity 5: Rock Explorations 80
Rocks rhyme 85
Rocks rhyme by lines 86
Upper- and lowercase matching letters for "rocks" 87
"Rocks" poem 88
"Rocks" by lines 89
Rocks pattern book pages 90
Readers Theatre: "Ten Little Rocks" 91
Readers Theatre: "I Found a Rock" 92
Pictures of large and small rocks 93

Activity 6: Flower Explorations 94
Flowers pattern 99
Flowers pattern by lines 100
Upper- and lowercase matching letters for "sunflower" 101
"Sunflower" poem 102
"Sunflower" by lines 103
Sunflower pattern book pages 104
"There's a Flower in the Middle of My Yard" poem 105
Pictures of large and small flowers 106

Activity 7: Chicken Soup with Rice 108
Soup rhyme 112
Soup rhyme by lines 113
Upper- and lowercase matching letters for "soup" 114
"Soup, Soup, Soup" poem 115
"Soup, Soup, Soup" by lines 116
Soup pattern book pages 117
Readers Theatre: "Making Chicken Soup" 118
Pictures of soup bowls and soup pots 119

Activity 8: Magnet Explorations 120
Magnets rhyme 125
Magnets rhyme by lines 126
Upper- and lowercase matching letters for "magnets" 127
"Magnets" poem 128
"Magnets" poem by lines 129
Magnet pattern book pages 130
Readers Theatre: "The Very Sticky Magnet" 131
Pictures of large and small magnets 132

Activity 9: Worm Races 133
"Worms" riddle 138
"Worms" riddle by lines 139
Upper- and lowercase matching letters for "earthworms" 140
"Nobody Likes Me" poem 141
"Nobody Likes Me" by lines 142
Readers Theatre: "The Apple and the Worm" 143
Pictures of worms 144

Activity 1
PINEAPPLE EXPLORATIONS

Materials
- Whole pineapple
- Pineapple juice
- Knife and cutting board (pineapple cutter optional)
- Paper plates, small cups, and napkins
- Wipes to clean hands
- Chart paper and a marking pen
- Student copies of rhyme (Emergent level, page 30) or poem (Beginning level, page 33)
- Copies of pineapple pictures (page 38, optional)

DAY 1
The Language Experience

Students taste the meat and core of a pineapple, and develop a dictation based on this experience and discussion. Beginning readers can compare the core with the meat of the pineapple. With Emergent readers you might want to simply focus on the meat of the pineapple.

- Pass the pineapple among the students. *"What do you notice about this pineapple? How does the skin feel? How does it smell? What colors do you see?"*
- Cut off the leaves and cut the pineapple in quarters lengthwise. *"What do you see inside of the pineapple? What new colors do you see?"*
- Cut away the core from each quarter piece and give students a piece. *"Touch the core. Chew the core but do not swallow it. Spit out the core into a napkin. How did the core feel in your mouth?"*
- Students taste the pineapple meat. *"How does the pineapple meat taste, feel, and smell?"*
- Give each student a small amount of pineapple juice in a clear cup. *"Hold the cup up to the light. Can you see through the juice? Smell the juice, then taste it. What do you notice?"*
- Students talk to a neighbor about what they learned. *"Think of three things to say about the pineapple and the juice."*

Chart the Experience
Chart and Read: *Emergent Readers*
- Encourage the small group to dictate a sentence about the experience. *"Let's write a sentence about the pineapple on our chart. What is the most important thing to say about the pineapple?"*

Pineapples

Pineapples are yellow and green.

Emergent reader chart sample

Students often focus on color. Help them to form a one-sentence dictation. Say each word as you write it.

- Reread the sentence and ask the students for a title.
- Record the title.
- Have the students choral read what's on the chart while you point to the words.
- Choral read while a student points to the words.
- Draw a simple pineapple on the chart or use the reproducible on page 38.

Chart and Read: *Beginning Readers*

- Have a large sheet of chart paper ready for writing students' sentences. *"Think about the sentence you want me to write on the chart."* As each student dictates a sentence, write it on the chart and repeat the words.
- Use names and color-code the sentences to help support Beginning readers.
- Read the chart to the group.
- Guide the group in deciding on a title. *"Now we have our sentences. I will read the chart. While I am reading it, I'd like you to think about what would make a good title. Let's get some ideas and then decide which one to use."* Record the title at the top of the chart.
- Choral read with the students while you point to the words.
- Choral read while a student points to the words.
- Draw a simple pineapple on the chart or use the reproducible on page 38.

Pineapples

Abbey said, "It was sticky and sweet."

Shawn said, "I liked the leaves growing out of the top."

Tiffany said, "It was a pretty yellow."

Roma said, "There were prickly things on the outside."

Kai said, "I like pineapples!"

Beginning reader chart sample

Instructions for making student copies of chart experience for rereading:

- Type the chart (using a 26- to 36-point font) and make copies for each student in the group.
- Be sure to leave an extra wide margin on the left side of the page for hole punching and space at the bottom of the page for a picture.
- Add: *Story* _____ on the upper left corner and *Date* _____ on the upper right corner.
- These typed charts will be used for rereading on subsequent days.

Chart and Read:
Middle/Late Beginning Readers

As students become more fluent readers, they will not need the support of color or names and will be able to reread paragraphs. Here is a sample of a lengthy GEC with late Beginning readers.

Pineapples

We ate a pineapple today. It looked like a big potato with sharp leaves at the top. It had prickly things on the outside that can pinch you.

We cut off the top and the bottom. Then we cut the hard skin off. The pineapple was yellow and juicy inside. We ate the yellow fruit. It was sticky and sweet. We drank some of the juice. It was sweet, too. We like pineapples!

Middle/Late Beginning reader chart sample

DAY 2
Rereading in the Personal Reader
Emergent and Beginning Readers

- Make a copy of the dictation for each student in the group. These typed Group Experience Charts will be used for rereading on subsequent days. (See page 25 for instructions.)
- Pass out the copies and have the students put them in their Personal Readers.
- Reread the chart to the group.
- Choral read while one or two students point to the words.
- Ask the students to point to and reread either their sentence or the whole chart.
- Have the students partner read the individual copies in their Personal Readers.
- Have them underline three or four known words on their copies and write the words at the bottom of the page.
- Have them draw a picture on their individual copies to help remember the text. For students who need additional support, have them draw a picture by each line.

DAYS 3–7
Extension Activities
Emergent Readers

1. Use the rhyme (to the right), and follow the process for rereading on Day 2. Give each student a copy (provided on page 30) to use as a reference when they rebuild the rhyme line by line.
2. Act out the rhyme or create a fingerplay.

Story # ______ Date ______

Pineapples

Pineapples, pineapples
Taste so fine!
Pineapples, pineapples
Want some of mine?

Color a box each time you read.

3. Using the blacklines on page 31, have students arrange the lines in order by matching them to the chart.

Pineapples

Pineapples, pineapples

Taste so fine!

Pineapples, pineapples

Want some of mine?

4. Have the students hunt for particular letters on the chart. Use Wikki Stix or highlighter tape to identify them.
5. Have the students match uppercase letters to lowercase letters. A student copy of the letters is provided on page 32.

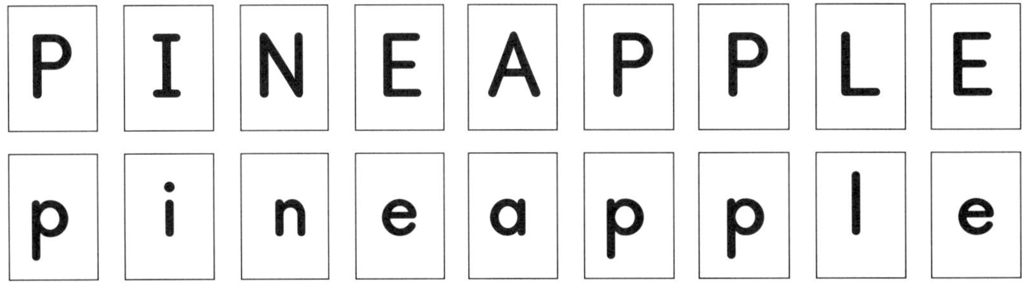

Beginning Readers

1. Use the poem (to the right), and follow the process for rereading on Day 2 (page 27). A student copy of the poem is provided on page 33.
   - Have the students choral read and buddy read the poem.
   - Have the students reread the poem using different voices, such as a whispery voice or a happy voice.
   - Ask the students to dramatize the poem. Put them in groups and have them present their dramatizations.
2. Make copies of the poem for students (see pages 34-35). Distribute one stanza to each student or pair of students. Have them cut apart the stanza into words or lines and then rebuild.
   - Extension: have each student or pair work on a different stanza.

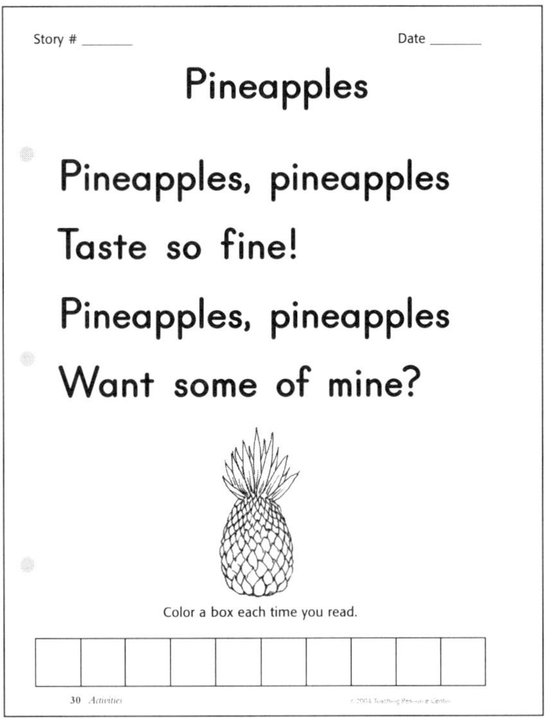
Story # ______ Date ______

Pineapples

Pineapples, pineapples

Taste so fine!

Pineapples, pineapples

Want some of mine?

Color a box each time you read.

3. Have the students use the pattern (Figure A) to create a class book or pages for the Personal Readers, on how they like to eat pineapples. A blackline is provided on page 36.
4. Add a Readers Theatre script to the Personal Reader. Below is a script we created (Figure B). A student copy of the script is provided on page 37.
5. Have the students hunt for words that begin with a certain letter or pattern that is developmentally appropriate. Beginning readers might hunt for:
   - known words
   - beginning and ending consonants
   - rhyming words
   - phonograms (word families)
   - blends and digraphs
   - short vowel CVC words
6. Have the students write what they now know about pineapples (Figure C).

Figure A

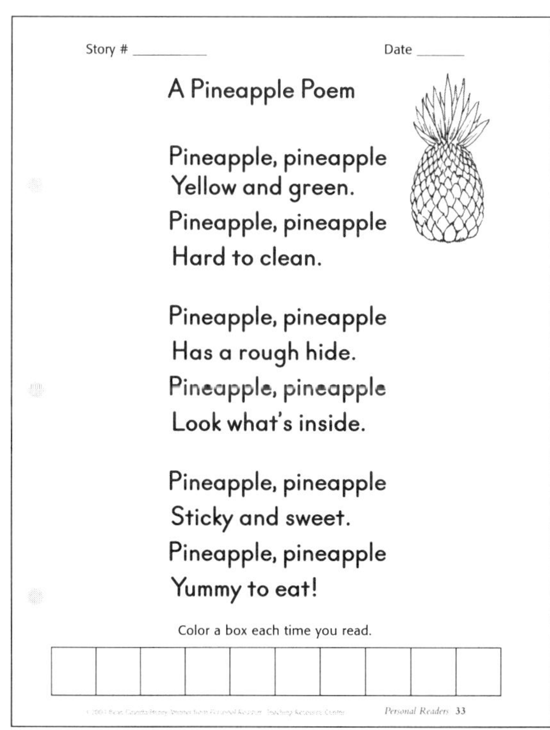

Story # ________ Date ______

A Pineapple Poem

Pineapple, pineapple
Yellow and green.
Pineapple, pineapple
Hard to clean.

Pineapple, pineapple
Has a rough hide.
Pineapple, pineapple
Look what's inside.

Pineapple, pineapple
Sticky and sweet.
Pineapple, pineapple
Yummy to eat!

Color a box each time you read.

Personal Readers 33

Figure B

Pineapples have leaves
growing out of the top.

Pineapples are yellow and green.

Pineapples have prickles on
the outside.

Pineapples have yellow fruit
on the inside.

Figure C

Story # _______ Date _______

Pineapples

Pineapples, pineapples
Taste so fine!
Pineapples, pineapples
Want some of mine?

Color a box each time you read.

Pineapples

Pineapples, pineapples

Taste so fine!

Pineapples, pineapples

Want some of mine?

P I N E A P

P L E p i n

e a p p l e

Story # __________ Date _______

A Pineapple Poem

Pineapple, pineapple
Yellow and green.
Pineapple, pineapple
Hard to clean.

Pineapple, pineapple
Has a rough hide.
Pineapple, pineapple
Look what's inside.

Pineapple, pineapple
Sticky and sweet.
Pineapple, pineapple
Yummy to eat!

Color a box each time you read.

Pineapple

Pineapple, pineapple
Yellow and green.
Pineapple, pineapple
Hard to clean.
Pineapple, pineapple
Has a rough hide.
Pineapple, pineapple
Look what's inside.

Pineapple, pineapple

Sticky and sweet.

Pineapple, pineapple

Yummy to eat!

I like to eat pineapples ________

____.

I like to eat pineapples ________

____.

Story # _______________ Date ________

Here Is a Pineapple

Reader 1:	Here is a pineapple
Reader 2:	Yellow and green.
Reader 1:	Here is a pineapple
Reader 2:	Ready to eat.
Reader 1:	Here is a pineapple
Reader 2:	Cut it in two.
Reader 1:	Here is a pineapple
Reader 2:	For me and you.

Color a box each time you read.

Activity 2

Bubble Explorations

Materials

- 1 gallon of water
- 1 cup of dish soap
- 40–60 drops of glycerin
- Large bowl
- 3–4 bubble wands of different shapes (or wire hangers bent into different shapes)
- Newspaper to cover work area
- Chart paper and a marking pen
- Student copies of rhyme (Emergent level, page 44) or poem (Beginning level, page 47)
- Copies of bubble pictures (page 53, optional)

DAY 1

The Language Experience

For best results mix the water, dish soap, and glycerin in front of the students at least one hour prior to the group experience. Instruct the students in dipping bubble wands into the soap solution and develop a dictation based on this experience and discussion.

- Place the bubble solution in the middle of the work area. Have the glycerin bottle, dish soap, and a glass of water available to remind students how the solution was made. *"Earlier today you watched me make the bubble solution. Now we are going to have an opportunity to create bubbles. Watch as I dip my wand into the bubble solution and carefully blow a bubble. In just a few minutes, you'll be able to blow a bubble too."*
- Before children take turns dipping their wands into the mixture, ask them to predict the shape of their bubble and remind them to blow slowly. *"What colors did you see in the bubble? Was your bubble round? Did we see any bubbles that were not round?"*
- Have the students switch wands with a neighbor and take another turn blowing a bubble. They can try to catch the bubble. *"What happened when you touched the bubble? What is inside the bubble?"*

Chart the Experience

Chart and Read: *Emergent Readers*

- Guide the small group in dictating a sentence about the experience. *"Let's write a sentence about bubbles on our chart. What is the most important thing to say about bubbles?"*

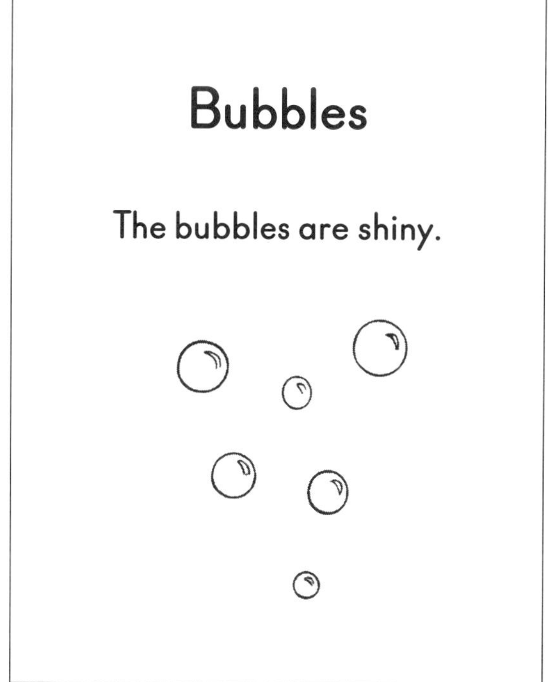

Emergent reader chart sample

Students often focus on color. Help them to form a one-sentence dictation. Say each word as you write it.
- Reread the sentence and ask the students for a title.
- Record the title.
- Choral read with the students while you point to the words.
- Choral read while a student points to the words.
- Draw some simple bubbles on the chart or use the reproducible on page 53.

Chart and Read: *Beginning Readers*

- Have a large sheet of chart paper ready for writing students' sentences. *"Think about the sentence you want me to write on the chart."* As each student dictates a sentence, write it on the chart and repeat it.
- Use names and color-code the sentences to help support Beginning readers.
- Read the chart to the group.
- Ask the group to decide on a title. *"Now we have our sentences. I will read the chart. While I am reading it, I'd like you to think about what would make a good title. Let's get some ideas and then decide which one to use."* Record the title at the top of the chart.
- Choral read with the students while you point to the words.
- Choral read while a student points to the words.
- Draw a few bubbles on the chart or use the reproducible on page 53.

Bubbles

Maria said, "My bubble popped."
Sergio said, "I liked watching my bubble float."
Jenni said, "I blew a big bubble with the big wand."
Nikki said, "I made two bubbles on top of each other."
Matt said, "There is just air inside the bubbles."

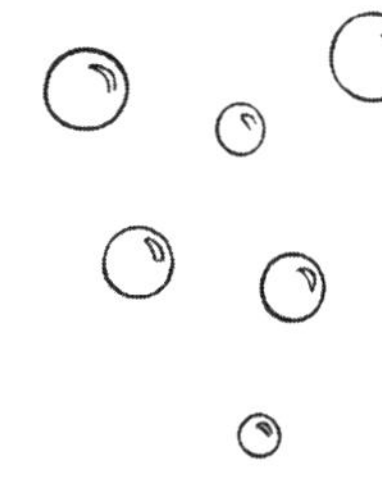

Beginning reader chart sample

Instructions for making student copies of chart experience for rereading:

- Type the chart (using a 26- to 36-point font) and make copies for each student in the group.
- Be sure to leave an extra wide margin on the left side of the page for hole punching and space at the bottom of the page for a picture.
- Add: *Story* _____ on the upper left corner and *Date* _____ on the upper right corner.
- These typed charts will be used for rereading on subsequent days.

Chart and Read:
Middle/Late Beginning Readers

As students become more fluent readers, they will not need the support of color or names and will be able to reread paragraphs.

Bubbles

Today we learned how to make bubbles. We used water, glycerin, and dish soap. We made small, round bubbles when we used the small, round wands. We got bigger bubbles when we used bigger wands. We thought we'd get different shaped bubbles when we used the triangle and square wands. That didn't happen. All the bubbles we made were round.

Some of our bubbles popped as we were making them. They just have air inside. Other bubbles floated up in the air before popping. They have lots of colors when you see them in the light. We are going to try making bubbles again tomorrow.

Middle/Late Beginning reader chart sample

DAY 2

Rereading in the Personal Reader

Emergent and Beginning Readers

- Make a copy of the dictation for each student in the group. These typed Group Experience Charts will be used for rereading on subsequent days. (See page 39 for instructions.)
- Pass out the copies and have the students put them in their Personal Readers.
- Reread the chart to the group.
- Choral read while one or two students point to the words.
- Ask the students to point to and reread either their sentence or the whole chart.
- Have the students partner read the individual copies in their Personal Readers.
- Have them underline three or four known words on their copies and write the words at the bottom of the page.
- Have them draw a picture on their individual copies to help remember the text. For students who need additional support, have them draw a picture by each line.

DAYS 3–7

Extension Activities

Emergent Readers

Use the rhyme (to the right), and follow the process for rereading on Day 2. Give each student a copy (provided on page 44) to use as a reference when they rebuild the rhyme line by line.

2. Act out the rhyme or create a fingerplay.

3. Using the blacklines on page 45, have students arrange the lines in order by matching them to the chart.

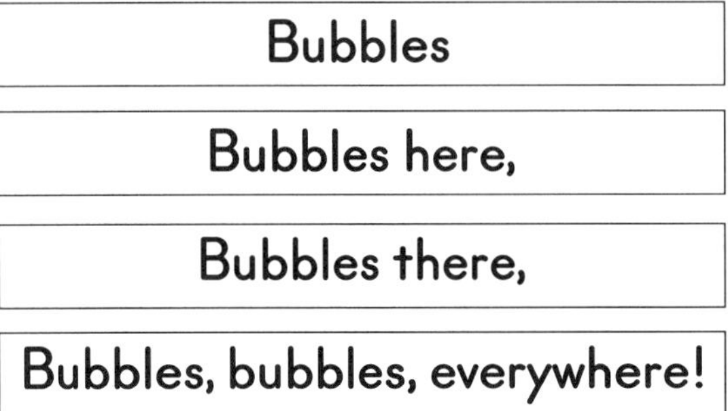

4. Have the students hunt for particular letters on the chart. Use Wikki Stix or highlighter tape to identify them.
5. Have the students match uppercase letters to lowercase letters. A student copy of the letters is provided on page 46.

Beginning Readers

1. Use the poem (to the right), and follow the process for rereading on Day 2 (page 41). A student copy of the poem is provided on page 47.
   - Have the students choral read and buddy read the poem.
   - Have the students reread the poem using different voices, such as a whispery voice or a happy voice.
   - Ask the students to dramatize the poem. Put them in groups and have them present their dramatizations.
2. Make copies of the poem for students (see page 48-49). Distribute one stanza to each student or pair of students. Have them cut apart the stanza into words or lines and then rebuild.
   - Extension: have each student or pair work on a different stanza.

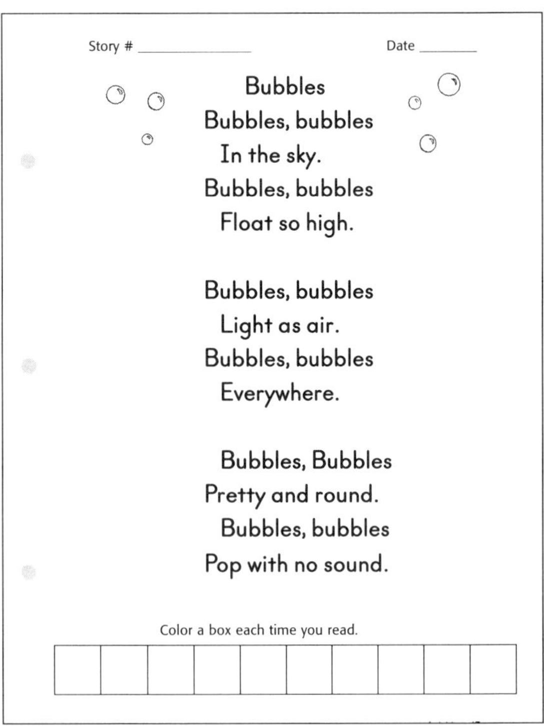
Story # ____________ Date ________

Bubbles

Bubbles, bubbles
In the sky.
Bubbles, bubbles
Float so high.

Bubbles, bubbles
Light as air.
Bubbles, bubbles
Everywhere.

Bubbles, Bubbles
Pretty and round.
Bubbles, bubbles
Pop with no sound.

Color a box each time you read.

3. Have the students use the "Bubbles can be ____" pattern to create individual books. A blackline for an eight-page book is provided on pages 51 and 52. Cut along the dotted lines to make four simple pattern books. Staple the pages at the top. Tell the students to open the cover and write an adjective to describe bubbles on the blank line (See Figure A).
4. Add a Readers Theatre script to the Personal Reader. Here is a script we created (Figure B). A student copy of the script is provided on page 50.
5. Have the students hunt for words that begin with a certain letter or pattern that is developmentally appropriate. Beginning readers might hunt for:
   - known words
   - beginning and ending consonants
   - rhyming words
   - phonograms (word families)
   - blends and digraphs
   - short vowel CVC words
6. Have the students write what they now know about bubbles (Figure C).

Figure A

Story # ________ Date ________

Bubbles

Reader 1: Bubbles, bubbles everywhere.

Reader 2: See them floating in the air.

Reader 1: Look inside. They're very clear.

Reader 2: Do it quick before they disappear!

Reader 1: Bubbles, bubbles in the room.

Reader 2: Try to catch them before they go

All: BOOM!

Color a box each time you read.

50 *Personal Readers*

Figure B

Bubbles are made with water, glycerin, and Dawn.

A bigger wand makes bigger bubbles.

Bubbles are always round.

Bubbles are a rainbow color.

Bubbles have air inside, and you can see through them.

Figure C

Story # ___________ Date _______

Bubbles

Bubbles here,

Bubbles there,

Bubbles, bubbles everywhere!

Color a box each time you read.

Bubbles

Bubbles here,

Bubbles there,

Bubbles, bubbles, everywhere!

B	U	B	B
L	E	S	
b	u	b	b
l	e	s	

Story # ___________ Date________

Bubbles

Bubbles, bubbles
In the sky.
Bubbles, bubbles
Float so high.

Bubbles, bubbles
Light as air.
Bubbles, bubbles
Everywhere.

Bubbles, bubbles
Pretty and round.
Bubbles, bubbles
Pop with no sound.

Color a box each time you read.

Bubbles

Bubbles, bubbles

In the sky.

Bubbles, bubbles

Float so high.

Bubbles, bubbles

Light as air.

Bubbles, bubbles

Everywhere.

Bubbles, bubbles

Pretty and round.

Bubbles, bubbles

Pop with no sound.

Story # ___________ Date ________

Bubbles

Reader 1: Bubbles, bubbles everywhere.

Reader 2: See them floating in the air.

Reader 1: Look inside. They're very clear.

Reader 2: Do it quick before they disappear!

Reader 1: Bubbles, bubbles in the room.

Reader 2: Try to catch them before they go

All: BOOM!

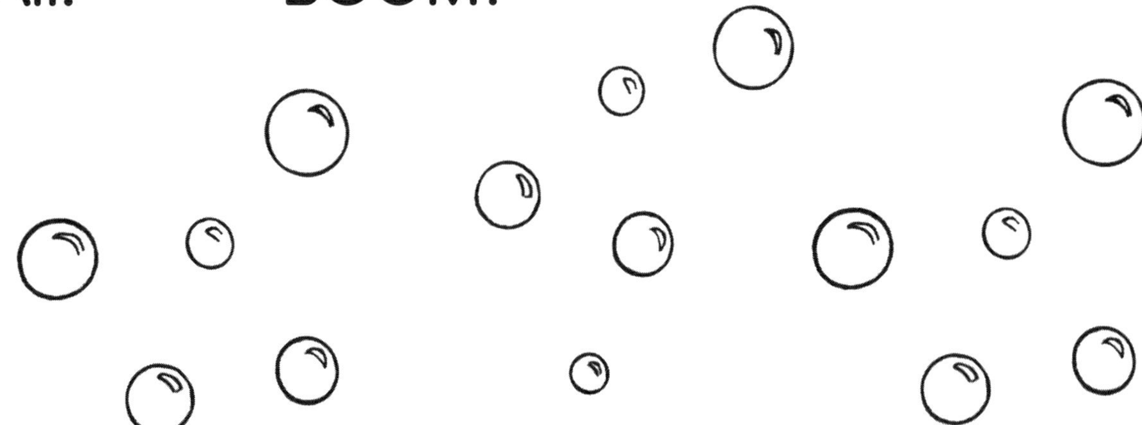

Color a box each time you read.

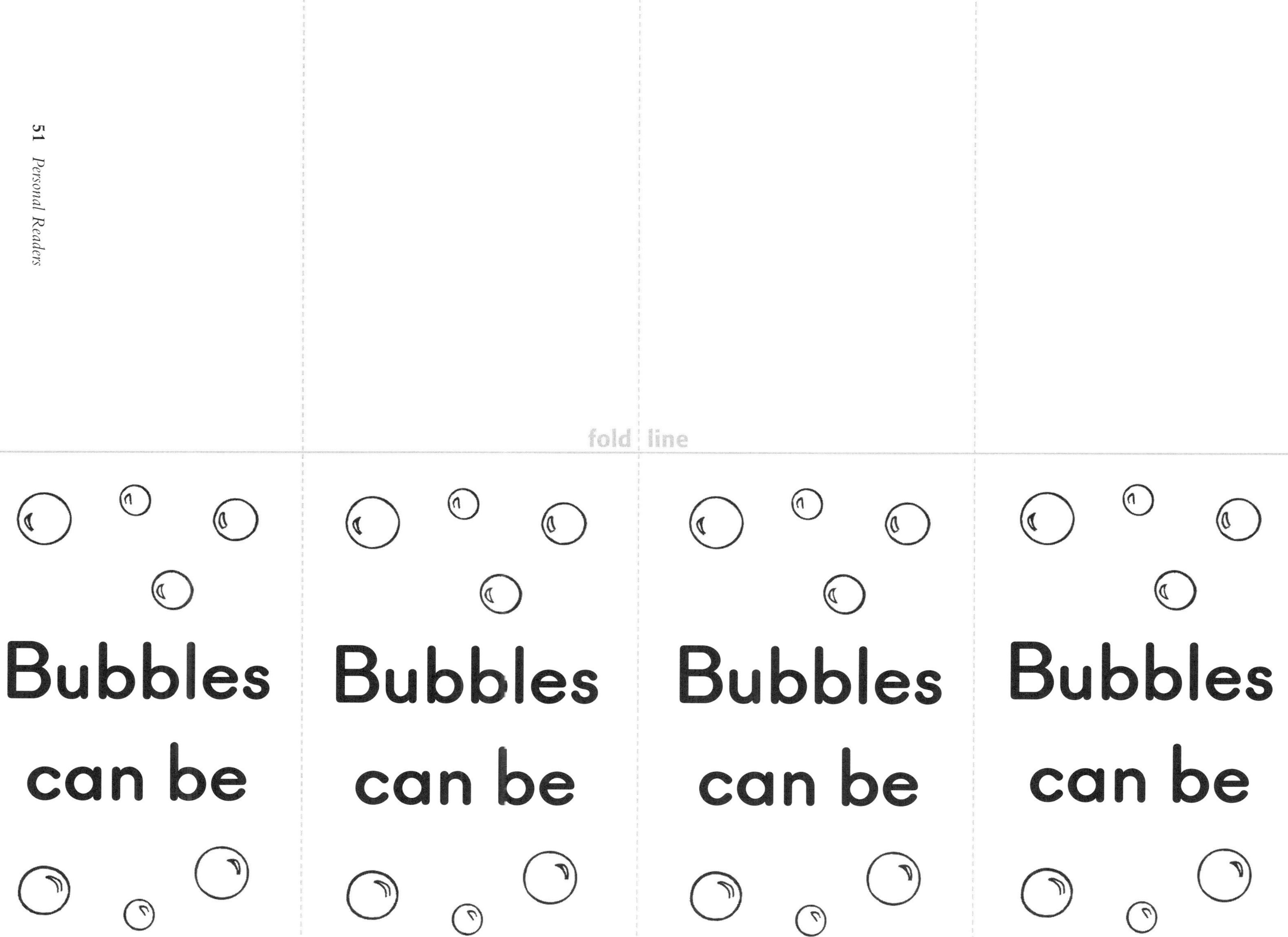
fold line
Bubbles can be
Bubbles can be
Bubbles can be
Bubbles can be

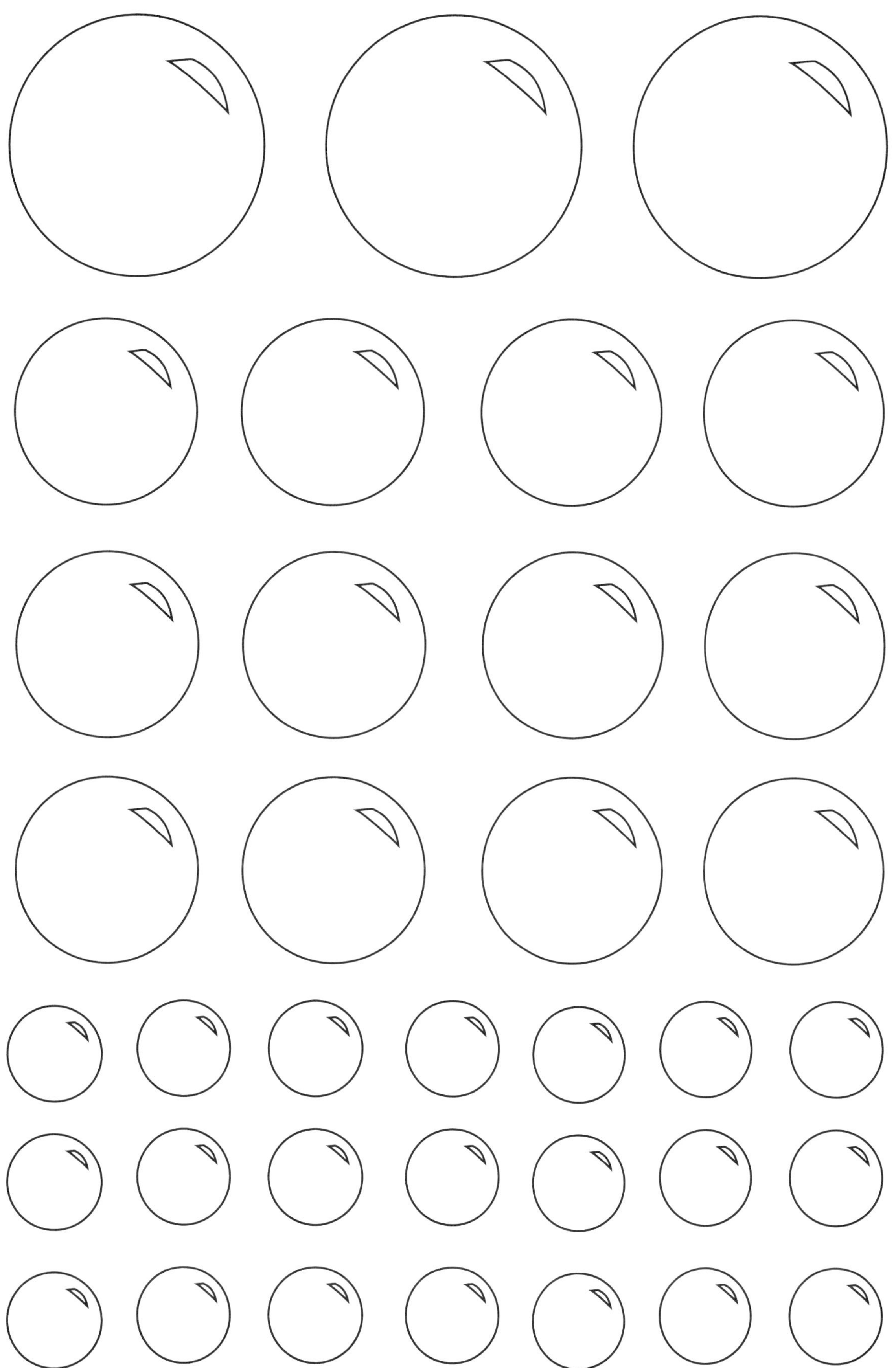

Activity 3

COLOR EXPLORATIONS

Materials

- *Mouse Paint* by Ellen Walsh
- 3 clear containers of yellow, red, and blue colored water
- Tempera paint (yellow, red, and blue)
- Paint brushes
- Newspaper to cover the work area
- Student copies of rhyme (Emergent level, page 59) or poem (Beginning level, page 62)
- Copies of mouse-shaped patterns for students to fill in with mixed paint (page 66)

DAY 1

The Language Experience

Have the students listen to the book *Mouse Paint* by Ellen Walsh. After reading the book demonstrate how primary colors can be used to make secondary colors. Following this demonstration, let the children mix the colors themselves to create secondary colors.

- Read aloud *Mouse Paint* by Ellen Walsh to the small group. At the part when the mice begin to mix colors, pause and ask the students to predict what color will be made. *"What color do you think the mice will make now?"*
- After reading aloud, show children the colored water. *"How can we change the color of the yellow water to make it orange? What color should we add to the red water to make it purple? If I put yellow food coloring in the blue water, what color will we have then?"*
- Provide three mouse patterns to each student. Reread *Mouse Paint*, stopping each time a new color is made by the mice to allow students to create the color using Tempera paint. A new mouse pattern should be used for each new color mixing. *"What happens when you add more red to the yellow? What happens if you add more yellow than red? What is your favorite color?"* Note: Late Beginning readers can be introduced to vocabulary words such as primary colors and secondary colors as part of the color mixing activity. They can also experiment with creating lighter and darker shades of secondary colors.

Emergent reader chart sample

Chart the Experience

Chart and Read: *Emergent Readers*

- Guide the small group in dictating a sentence about the experience. *"Let's decide on a sentence to write on our chart about the colors. What is the most important thing to say about mixing the colors?"*

Help them to form a one-sentence dictation. Say each word as you write it.

- Reread the sentence and ask the students for a title.
- Record the title.
- Point to words as students reread the chart.
- Choral read with the students while you point to the words.
- Choral read while a student points to the words.
- Paint some color splotches on the chart paper, or use the reproducible on page 66.

Chart and Read:
Beginning Readers

- Have a large sheet of chart paper ready for writing students' sentences. *"Think about the sentence you want me to write on the chart."* As each student dictates a sentence, write it on the chart and repeat the words.
- Use names and color-code the sentences to help support Beginning readers.
- Read the chart to the group.
- Ask the group to decide on a title. *"Now we have our sentences. I will read the chart. While I am reading it, I'd like you to think about what would make a good title. Let's get some ideas and then decide which one to use."* Record the title at the top of the chart.
- Choral read with the students while you point to the words.
- Choral read while a student points to the words.
- Draw circles of color on the chart or use the reproducible on page 66.

Mixing Colors

Carly said, "I put yellow and blue paint together to make green paint."
Juan said, "The red water turned purple."
Rosita said, "I liked making orange paint."
Kristina said, "Red and blue turned into purple."

Beginning reader chart sample

Instructions for making student copies of chart experience for rereading:

- Type the chart (using a 26- to 36-point font) and make copies for each student in the group.
- Be sure to leave an extra wide margin on the left side of the page for hole punching and space at the bottom of the page for a picture.
- Add: *Story* _____ on the upper left corner and *Date* _____ on the upper right corner.
- These typed charts will be used for rereading on subsequent days.

Chart and Read:

Middle/Late Beginning Readers

As students become more fluent readers, they will not need the support of color or names and will be able to reread paragraphs.

Mixing Colors

After we read Mouse Paint we mixed the colors together like the mice in the story. We mixed yellow and blue to make green. When we mixed red and blue, the paint turned purple. Then we made orange by mixing yellow and red. We learned that yellow, red and blue are called primary colors. The other colors are called secondary colors.

Middle/Late Beginning reader chart sample

DAY 2

Rereading in the Personal Reader

Emergent and Beginning Readers

- Make a copy of the dictation for each student in the group. These typed Group Experience Charts will be used for rereading on subsequent days (see page 54 for instructions).
- Pass out the copies and have the students put them in their Personal Readers.
- Reread the chart to the group.
- Choral read while one or two students point to the words.
- Ask the students to point to and reread either their sentence or the whole chart.
- Have the students partner read the individual copies in their Personal Readers.
- Have them underline three or four known words on their copies and write the words at the bottom of the page.
- Have them draw a picture on their individual copies to help remember the text. For students who need additional support, have them draw a picture by each line.

Story # ____________ Date ________

Catch a Rainbow!

Red, blue, yellow and green
Catching a rainbow is my dream.

Red, blue, yellow and green,
I followed the rainbow color beam.

Red, blue, yellow and green,
Now the rainbow can't be seen!

Color a box each time you read.

DAYS 3–7

Extension Activities

Emergent Readers

1. Use the rhyme (to the right), which is based on the pattern found in *The Jigaree* by Joy Cowley. Follow the process for rereading on Day 2. Give each student a copy (provided on page 59) to use as a reference when they rebuild the rhyme line by line.
2. Act out the rhyme or create a fingerplay.

3. Using the blacklines on page 60, have students arrange the lines in order by matching them to the chart.

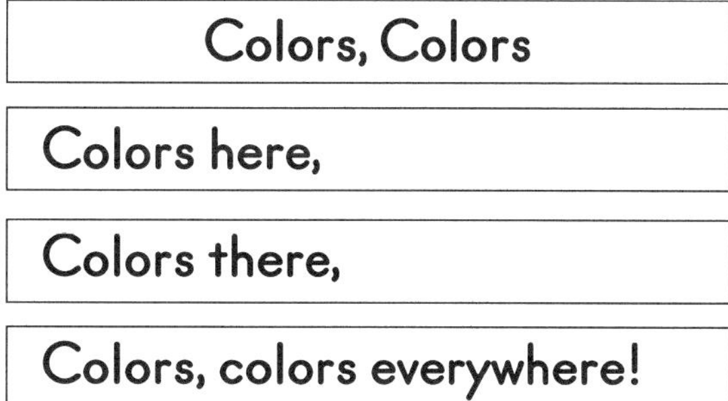

4. Have the students hunt for particular letters on the chart. Use Wikki Stix or highlighter tape to identify them.
5. Have the students match uppercase letters to lowercase letters. A student copy of the letters is provided on page 61.

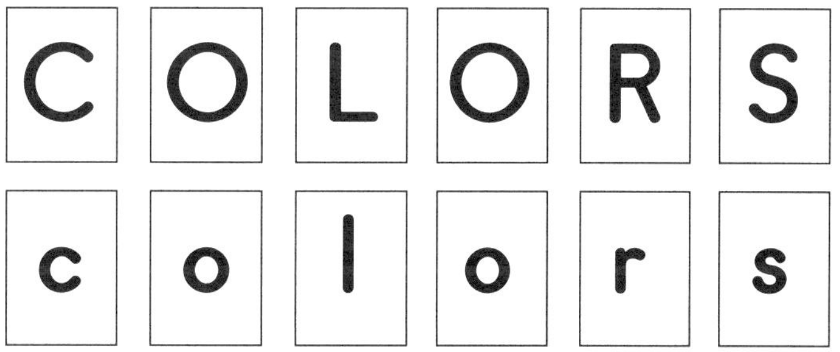

Beginning Readers

1. Use the poem (to the right), and follow the process for rereading on Day 2 (page 56). A student copy of the poem is provided on page 62.

- Have the students choral read and buddy read the poem.
  - Have the students reread the poem using different voices, such as a whispery voice or a happy voice.
  - Ask the students to dramatize the poem. Put them in groups and have them present their dramatizations.

2. Make copies of the poem for students (see page 63). Distribute one stanza to each student or pair of students. Have them cut apart the stanza into words or lines and then rebuild.
   - Extension: have each student or pair work on a different stanza.

Story # ______________ Date ________

Magic in the Sky

Reader 1: Red in the sky
Reader 2: Orange in the sky
Reader 3: Yellow in the sky
Reader 4: Green in the sky
Reader 5: Blue in the sky
Reader 6: Purple in the sky
All: We made magic in the sky!

Color a box each time you read.

3. Have the students use the pattern (Figure A) to create a class book or pages for the Personal Reader. Each student can draw a picture to represent a favorite color.
4. Add a Readers Theatre script to the Personal Reader. Below is a script we created (Figure B). A student copy of the script is provided on page 65. Make a large rainbow out of felt or laminated paper. Each student in the group can have one color to use in building the rainbow. The rainbow can be displayed on a bulletin board along with the words of the Readers Theatre (see Figure B).

My favorite color is green.

Activities 61

Figure A

5. Have the students hunt for words that begin with a certain letter or pattern that is developmentally appropriate for beginning readers. Beginning readers might hunt for:
   - known words
   - beginning and ending consonants
   - rhyming words
   - phonograms (word families)
   - blends and digraphs
   - short vowel CVC words
6. Have the students write what they now know about colors (see Figure C).

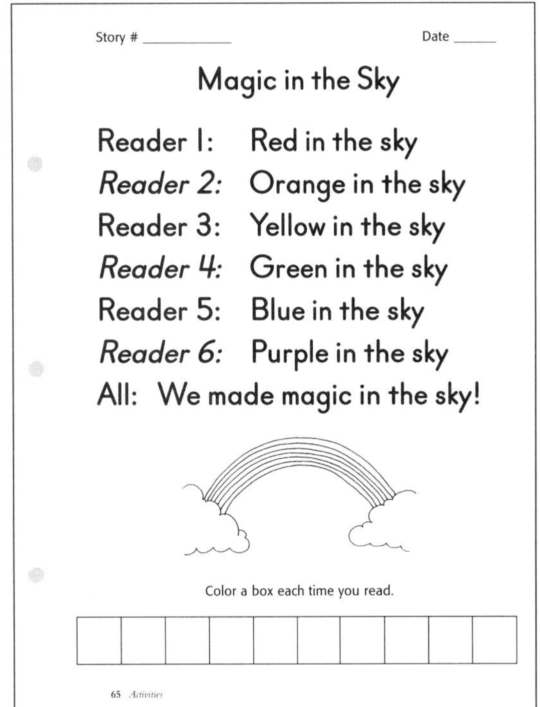
Story # ________ Date ______

Magic in the Sky

Reader 1: Red in the sky
Reader 2: Orange in the sky
Reader 3: Yellow in the sky
Reader 4: Green in the sky
Reader 5: Blue in the sky
Reader 6: Purple in the sky
All: We made magic in the sky!

Color a box each time you read.

65 Activities

Figure B

Mix red and blue paint to make purple.
Mix yellow and blue paint to make green.
Mix yellow and red paint to make orange.
Adding more yellow paint makes the color lighter.
All colors are made with red, yellow, and blue.

Figure C

Story # ______________ Date ______

Colors, Colors

Colors here,

Colors there,

Colors, colors everywhere!

Color a box each time you read.

Colors, Colors

Colors here,

Colors there,

Colors, colors everywhere!

C O L O R S

c o l o r s

Story # __________ Date __________

Catch a Rainbow!

Red, blue, yellow, and green
Catching a rainbow is my dream.

Red, blue, yellow, and green
I followed the rainbow color beam.

Red, blue, yellow, and green
Now the rainbow can't be seen!

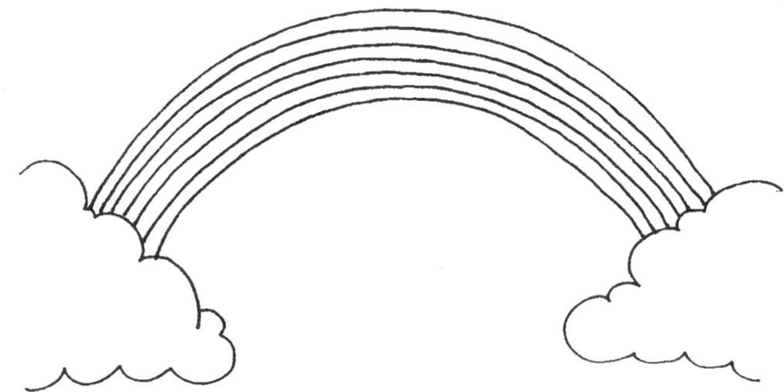

Color a box each time you read.

Catch a Rainbow

Red, blue, yellow, and green

Catching a rainbow is my dream.

Red, blue, yellow, and green

I followed the rainbow color beam.

Red, blue, yellow, and green

Now the rainbow can't be seen!

My favorite color is __________.

My favorite color is __________.

Story # ____________ Date ______

Magic in the Sky

Reader 1: Red in the sky

Reader 2: Orange in the sky

Reader 3: Yellow in the sky

Reader 4: Green in the sky

Reader 5: Blue in the sky

Reader 6: Purple in the sky

All: We made magic in the sky!

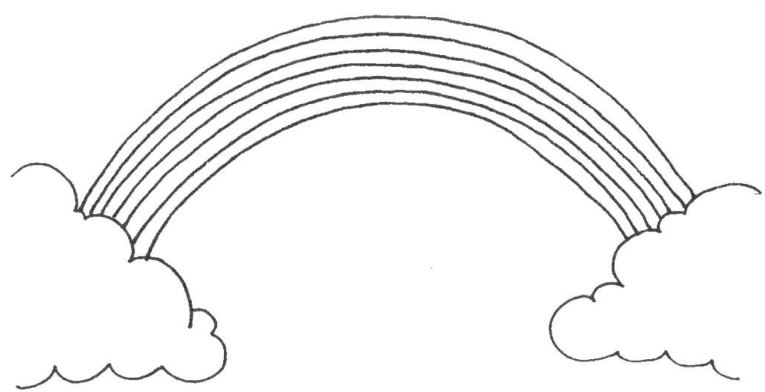

Color a box each time you read.

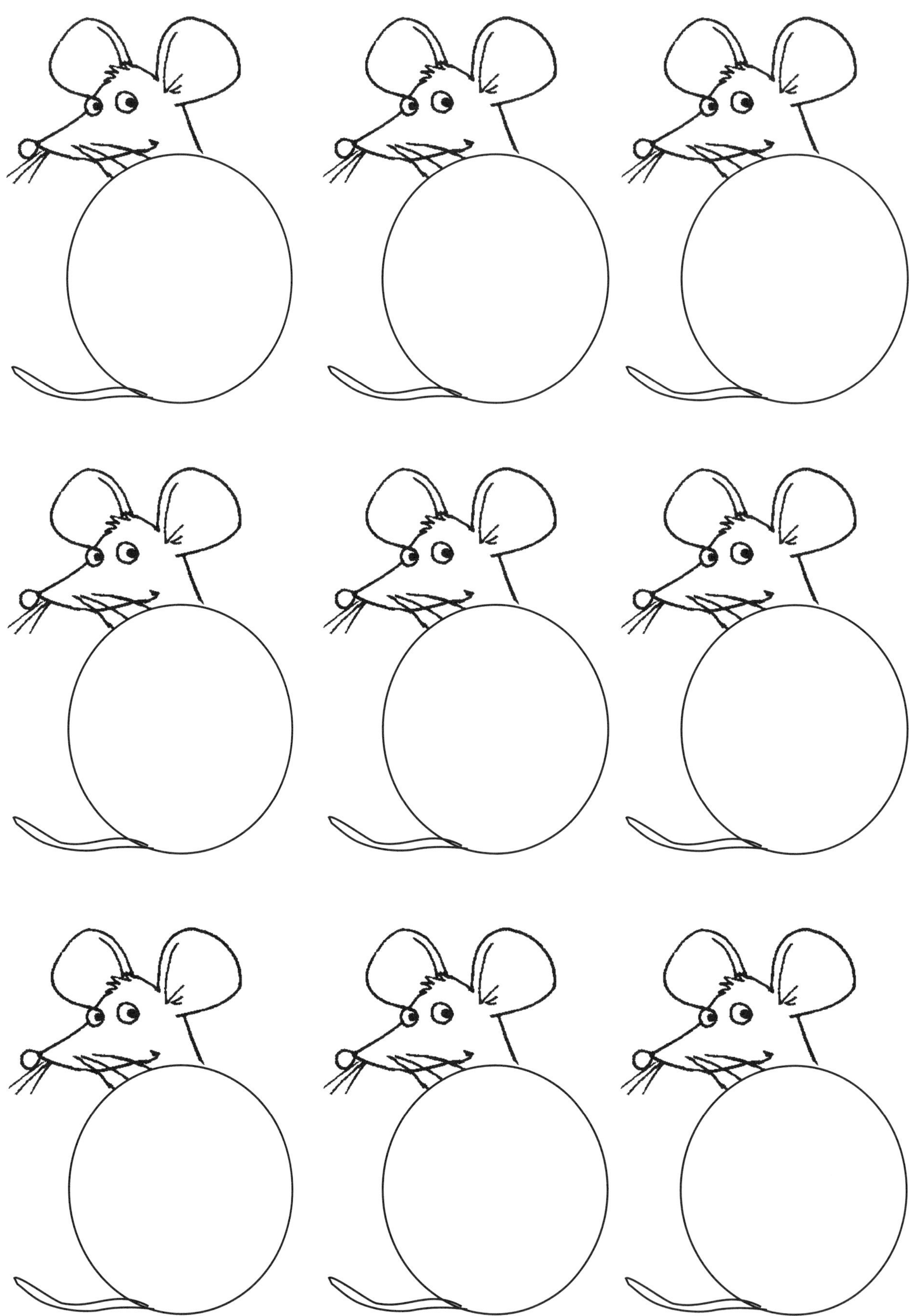

Activity 4

PIPE CLEANER FISH

Materials

- Pipe cleaners of various sizes, colors, and thicknesses
- Packing popcorn (or any sort of odd shaped Styrofoam pieces)
- Chart paper and marking pen
- Student copies of rhyme (Emergent level, page 72) or poem (Beginning level, page 75)
- Copies of fish pictures (page 79, optional)

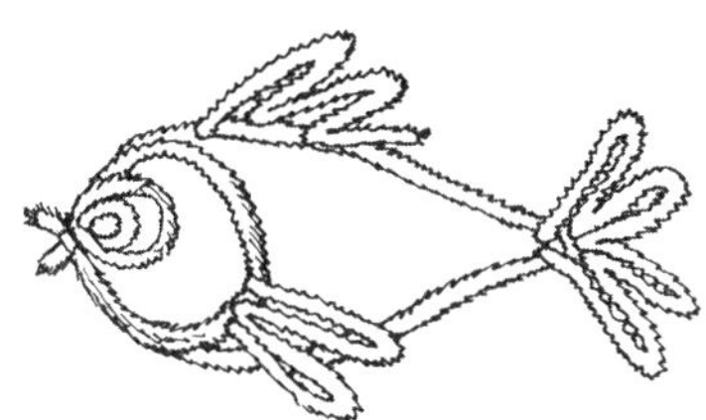

DAY 1

The Language Experience

Have the students create unique fish out of pipe cleaners and Styrofoam pieces, and develop a dictation based on this experience and discussion. Emergent readers should create one fish as a group. Beginning readers can each make a fish with a partner.

- Tell students they will be creating special fish and start a discussion. *"What can you tell me about fish? What makes different fish special?"* Show the group one or two samples of finished pipe cleaner fish. *"Here are some examples of fish made by other students."* Give the name of each fish and what made it special.
- Pass out two pipe cleaners and some packing popcorn to each student. Have the students create a special fish with the group or with their partner. Give students about 5 minutes to work together. *"Think about what you might create if you were going to make a special fish. You will be allowed to use the pipe cleaners and packing popcorn any way you want. Once you have created a fish, you can give the fish a name and think about what makes your fish special."*
- After the students have made their fish, have the partners or groups share information about the fish with everyone. If the students are working in partners, encourage them to talk about their fish's name, what makes their fish special, and what they like about their fish. Let them know about this part ahead of time. *"Be prepared to share your fish with the group. Tell us your fish's name and what makes it special or unique. Think about what you want written on the chart."*

Chart the Experience

Chart and Read: *Emergent Readers*

- Guide the small group in dictating a sentence about the experience. *"Let's write a sentence on our chart about this fish we made. What makes it special?"*

Emergent reader chart sample

Help them to form a one-sentence dictation. Say each word as you write it.

- Reread the sentence and ask the students for a title.
- Record the title.
- Point to words as the students reread the chart.
- Choral read with the students while you point to the words.
- Choral read while a student points to the words.
- Draw a simple fish on the chart or use the reproducible fish on page 79.

Chart and Read: *Beginning Readers*

- Have a large sheet of chart paper ready for writing students' sentences. *"Think about the sentence you want me to write on the chart."* As each student or pair dictates a sentence, write it on the chart and say each word as it is being written.
- Use names and color-code the sentences to help support Beginning readers.
- Read the chart to the group.
- Ask the group to decide on a title. *"Now we have our sentences. I will read the chart. While I am reading it, I'd like you to think about what would make a good title. Let's get some ideas and then decide which one to use."* Record the title at the top of the chart.
- Choral read with the students while you point to the words.
- Choral read while a student points to the words.
- Draw a simple fish on the chart or use the reproducible fish on page 79.

Pipe Cleaner Fish

Avory said, "My fish can change colors."

Ling said, "Boo Fish scares away sharks."

Abbey said, "Happy Fish makes other fish laugh."

Roma said, "Book Fish likes to read books."

Damon said, "Hook Fish has a hook to catch seaweed."

Beginning reader chart sample

Instructions for making student copies of chart experience for rereading:

- Type the chart (using a 26- to 36-point font) and make copies for each student in the group.
- Be sure to leave an extra wide margin on the left side of the page for hole punching and space at the bottom of the page for a picture.
- Add: *Story* _____ on the upper left corner and *Date* _____ on the upper right corner.
- These typed charts will be used for rereading on subsequent days.

Chart and Read: *Middle/Late Beginning Readers*

As students become more fluent readers, they will not need the support of color or names and will be able to reread paragraphs.

Pipe Cleaner Fish

We made pipe cleaner fish today. We used pipe cleaners and foam popcorn to create our fish. It was fun to work with partners. All of the groups came up with different fish. Some were big and some were small. They were funny and scary.

After we were done making our fish we had to come up with a name. We also had to think about what made our fish special. The names helped to describe what was special about our fish.

We all had a good time making pipe cleaner fish. They are now hanging from the ceiling in our room with tags that tell about each fish.

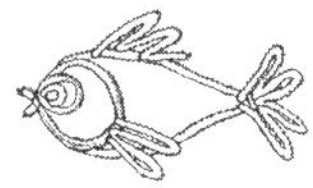

Middle/Late Beginning reader chart sample

DAY 2

Rereading in the Personal Reader

Emergent and Beginning Readers

- Make a copy of the dictation for each student in the group. These typed Group Experience Charts will be used for rereading on subsequent days. (See page 67 for instructions.)
- Pass out the copies and have the students put them in their Personal Readers.
- Reread the chart to the group.
- Choral read while one or two students point to the words.
- Ask the students to point to and reread either their sentence or the whole chart.
- Have the students partner read the individual copies in their Personal Readers.
- Have them underline three or four known words on their copies and write the words at the bottom of the page.
- Have them draw a picture on their individual copies to help remember the text. For students who need additional support, have them draw a picture by each line.

DAY 3–7

Extension Activities

Emergent Readers

1. Use the rhyme (to the right), and follow the process for rereading on Day 2. Give each student a copy (provided on page 72) to use as a reference when they rebuild the rhyme line by line.
2. Act out the rhyme or create a fingerplay.

Story # __________ Date ______

Fishy, Fishy

Fishy, Fishy,
In the sea.
Fishy, Fishy,
Swim with me.

Color a box each time you read.

72 Activities

3. Using the blacklines on page 73, have students arrange the lines in order by matching them to the chart.

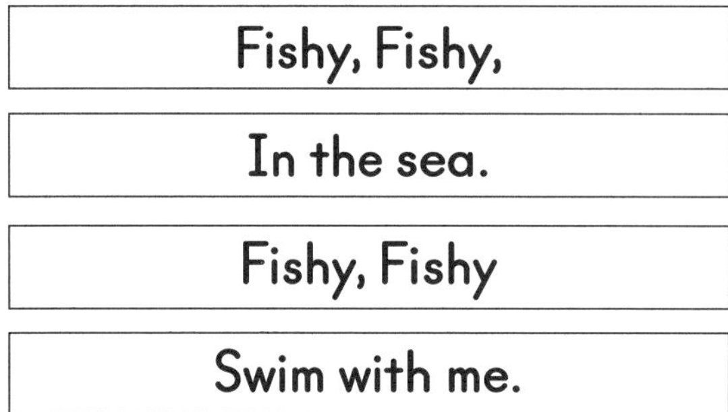

4. Have the students hunt for particular letters on the chart. Use Wikki Stix or highlighter tape to identify them.
5. Have the students match uppercase letters to lowercase letters. A student copy is provided on page 74.

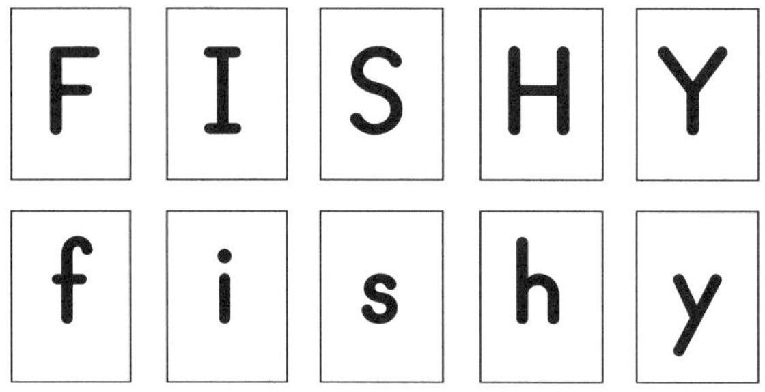

Beginning Readers

1. Use the poem (to the right), and follow the process for rereading on Day 2 (page 69). A student copy of the poem is provided on page 75.
- Have the students choral read and buddy read the poem.
  - Have the students reread the poem using different voices, such as a whispery voice or a happy voice.
  - Ask the students to dramatize the poem. Put them in groups and have them present their dramatizations.
2. Make copies of the poem for students (see page 76). Distribute one stanza to each student or pair of students. Have them cut apart the stanza into words or lines and then rebuild.
   - Extension: have each student or pair work on a different stanza.

Story # ____________ Date ______

I'm a Tiny Fishy

I'm a tiny fishy
In the sea.
Here are my fins,
Look at me.

When I want to have fun
With my friends,
I wiggle my tail
And play with glee!

Color a box each time you read.

Activities 75

3. Have the students use the pattern (Figure A) to create a class book or pages for the Personal Reader. A student copy is provided on page 77.
4. Add a Readers Theatre script to the Personal Reader. Below is a script we created (Figure B). A student copy of the script is provided on page 78.
5. Have the students hunt for words that begin with a certain letter or pattern that is developmentally appropriate. Beginning readers might hunt for:
   - known words
   - beginning and ending consonants
   - rhyming words
   - phonograms (word families)
   - blends and digraphs
   - short vowel CVC words
6. Have the students write what they now know about fish (Figure C).

Figure A

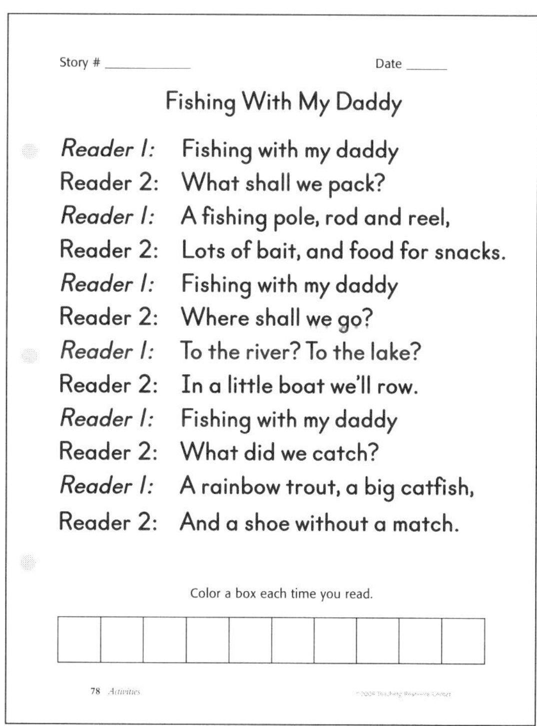

Story # ____________ Date ______

Fishing With My Daddy

Reader 1: Fishing with my daddy
Reader 2: What shall we pack?
Reader 1: A fishing pole, rod and reel,
Reader 2: Lots of bait, and food for snacks.
Reader 1: Fishing with my daddy
Reader 2: Where shall we go?
Reader 1: To the river? To the lake?
Reader 2: In a little boat we'll row.
Reader 1: Fishing with my daddy
Reader 2: What did we catch?
Reader 1: A rainbow trout, a big catfish,
Reader 2: And a shoe without a match.

Color a box each time you read.

78 *Activities*

Figure B

Figure C

Story # ____________ Date ______

Fishy, Fishy

Fishy, Fishy,
In the sea.
Fishy, Fishy,
Swim with me.

Color a box each time you read.

Fishy, Fishy,

Fishy, Fishy,

In the sea.

Fishy, Fishy,

Swim with me.

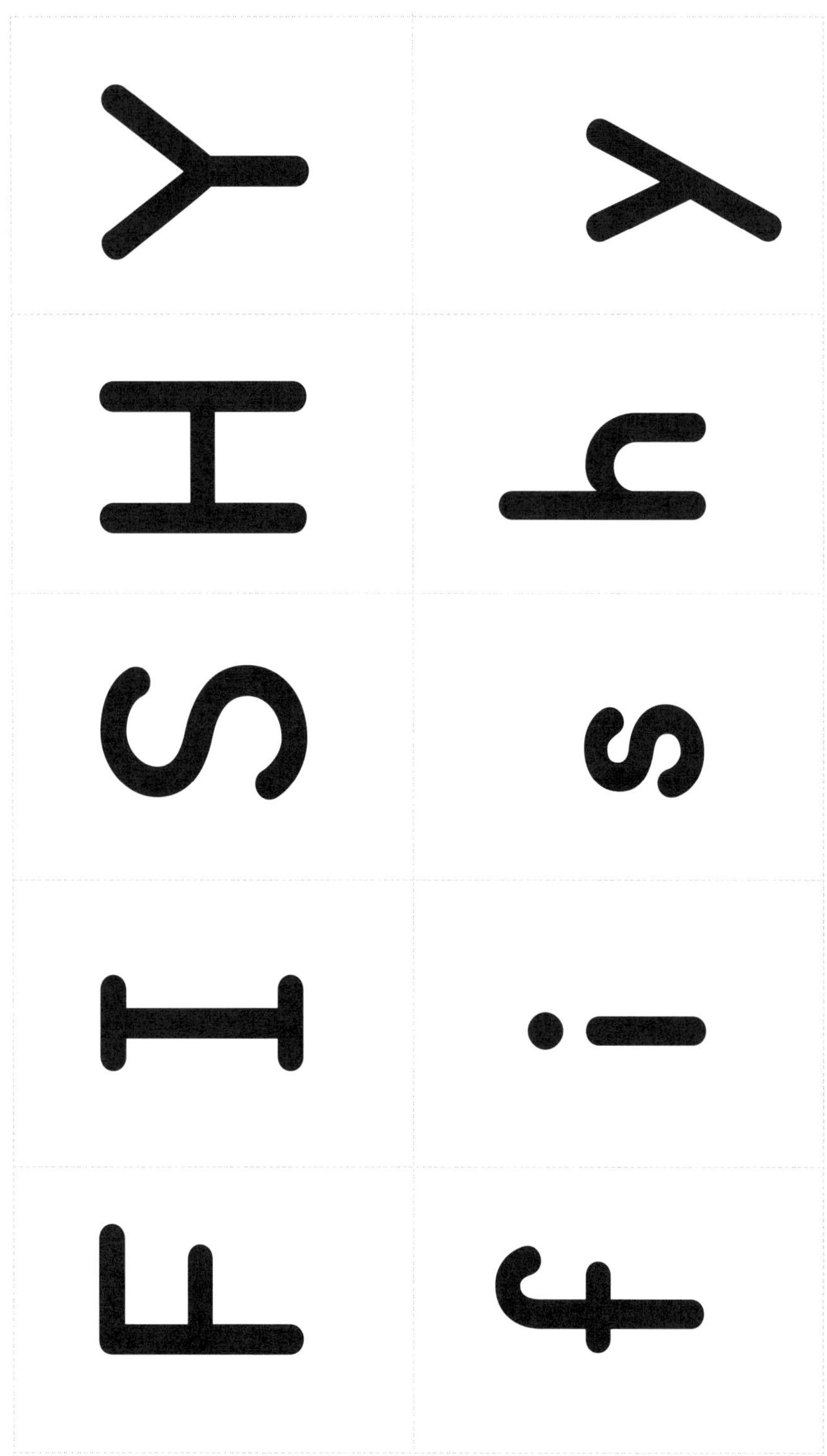
Y
y
H
h
S
s
I
i
F
f

Story # ____________ Date ______

I'm a Tiny Fishy

I'm a tiny fishy
In the sea.
Here are my fins,
Look at me.

When I want to have fun
With my friends,
I wiggle my tail
And play with glee!

Color a box each time you read.

I'm a Tiny Fishy

I'm a tiny fishy
In the sea.
Here are my fins,
Look at me.
When I want to have fun
With my friends,
I wiggle my tail
And play with glee!

The fish is ______________ .

The fish is ______________ .

Story # ____________ Date ______

Fishing With My Daddy

Reader 1: Fishing with my daddy
Reader 2: What shall we pack?
Reader 1: A fishing pole, rod and reel,
Reader 2: Lots of bait, and food for snacks.
Reader 1: Fishing with my daddy
Reader 2: Where shall we go?
Reader 1: To the river? To the lake?
Reader 2: In a little boat we'll row.
Reader 1: Fishing with my daddy
Reader 2: What did we catch?
Reader 1: A rainbow trout, a big catfish,
Reader 2: And a shoe without a match.

Color a box each time you read.

Activity 5
Rock Explorations

Materials

- A variety of rocks
- Magnifying glasses (hand-held)
- Chart paper and a marking pen
- Student copies of rhyme (Emergent level, page 85) or poem (Beginning level, page 88)
- Copies of rock pictures (page 93, optional)

DAY 1

The Language Experience

Have the students examine a variety of rocks and develop a dictation based on this experience. They will enjoy using magnifying glasses to look at the rocks in more detail.

- Have students share what they know about rocks. *"Today we are going to be looking at some rocks. Before we do, what can you tell us about rocks? Do any of you collect rocks? Tell us about it."*
- Put several different types of rocks out on the table for the students to examine and discuss. The discussion before the actual writing is very important. *"Here are some rocks to explore. What do you notice about them?"*
- Encourage the students to feel the rocks and describe what they are feeling. *"How do the rocks feel? Are they rough or smooth?"*
- Provide each student with a hand-held magnifying glass. *"Pick a rock that looks interesting to you. Use your magnifying glass to study it. We will share with the group what you noticed about your rock."*
- Allow students to look at other rocks with the magnifying glasses. *"Pass your rocks around and look at them with the magnifying glass. If you notice something about a rock that hasn't been said, share it with us."*
- Collect the rocks and magnifying glasses. Put the rocks on display. *"Talk to your neighbor about the rocks you examined today."*

Chart the Experience

Chart and Read: *Emergent Readers*

- Guide the small group in dictating a sentence about the experience. *"Let's write a sentence about rocks on our chart. What is the most important thing to say about the rocks?"* Students often focus on size. Help them to form a one-sentence dictation. Say each word as you write it.

Rocks

Some are big and some are small.

Emergent reader chart sample

- Reread the sentence and ask the students for a title.
- Record the title.
- Point to words as students reread the chart.
- Choral read with the students while you point to the words.
- Choral read while a student points to the words.
- Draw a simple rock on the chart or use the reproducible on page 93.

Chart and Read: *Beginning Readers*

- Have a large sheet of chart paper ready for writing students' sentences. *"Think about the sentence you want me to write on the chart."* As each student dictates a sentence, write it on the chart and repeat the words.
- Use names and color-code the sentences to help support Beginning readers.
- Read the chart to the group.
- Ask the group to decide on a title. *"Now we have our sentences. I will read the chart. While I am reading it, I'd like you to think about what would make a good title. Let's get some ideas and then decide which one to use."* Record the title at the top of the chart.
- Choral read with the students while you point to the words.
- Choral read while a student points to the words.
- Draw a simple rock on the chart or use the reproducible on page 93.

All About Rocks

Anahy said, "They're different shapes."
Rosa said, "The rocks feel heavy."
Avory said. "Some rocks are big, and some are small."
Kai said, "Some of them are bumpy."

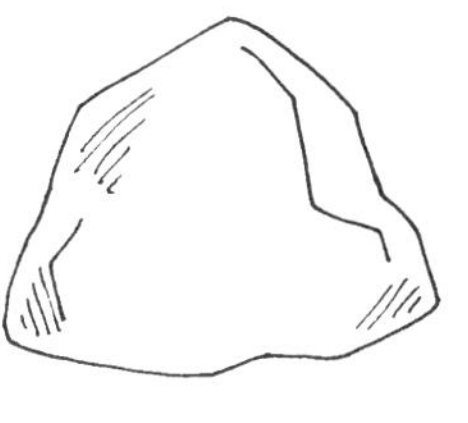

Beginning reader chart sample

Instructions for making student copies of chart experience for rereading:

- Type the chart (using a 26- to 36-point font) and make copies for each student in the group.
- Be sure to leave an extra wide margin on the left side of the page for hole punching and space at the bottom of the page for a picture.
- Add: *Story* _____ on the upper left corner and *Date* _____ on the upper right corner.
- These typed charts will be used for rereading on subsequent days.

Chart and Read:
Middle/Late Beginning Readers

As students become more fluent readers, they will not need the support of color or names and will be able to reread paragraphs.

Rocks

Today we looked at rocks. Some were big and some were small. We got to use magnifying glasses to look at them. It was fun. There were lots of stripes, holes, and bumps in the rocks. They were different colors, too. Some of the rocks were smooth and some were bumpy. We are going to bring in more rocks to look at tomorrow.

Middle/Late Beginning reader chart sample

DAY 2

Rereading in the Personal Reader

Emergent and Beginning Readers

- Make a copy of the dictation for each student in the group. These typed Group Experience Charts will be used for rereading on subsequent days. (See page 80 for instructions.)
- Pass out the copies and have the students put them in their Personal Readers.
- Reread the chart to the group.
- Choral read while one or two students point to the words.
- Ask the students to point to and reread either their sentence or the whole chart.
- Have the students partner read the individual copies in their Personal Readers.
- Have them underline three or four known words on their copies and write the words at the bottom of the page.
- Have them draw a picture on their individual copies to help remember the text. For students who need additional support, have them draw a picture by each line.

DAYS 3–7

Extension Activities

Emergent Readers

1. Use the rhyme (to the right), and follow the process for rereading on Day 2. Give each student a copy (provided on page 85) to use as a reference when they rebuild the rhyme line by line.
2. Act out the rhyme or create a fingerplay.

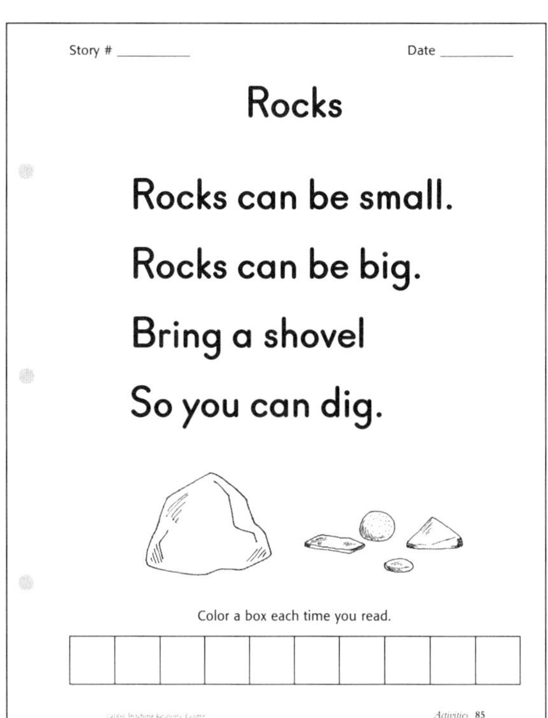

Story # ________ Date ________

Rocks

Rocks can be small.
Rocks can be big.
Bring a shovel
So you can dig.

Color a box each time you read.

Activities 85

3. Using the blacklines on page 86, have students arrange the lines in order by matching them to the chart.

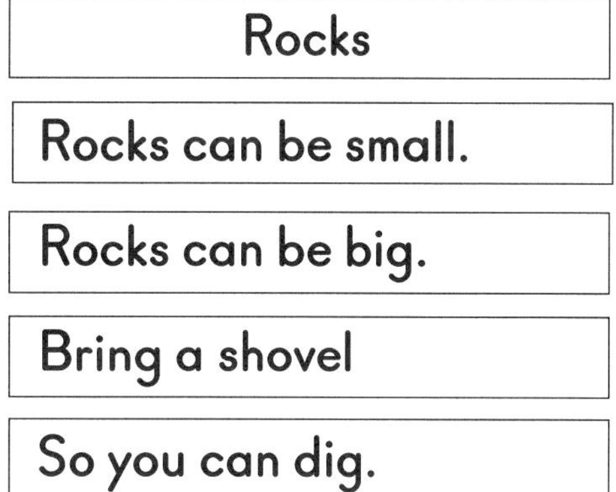

4. Have the students hunt for particular letters on the chart. Use Wikki Stix or highlighter tape to identify them.
5. Have the students match uppercase letters to lowercase letters. A student copy is provided on page 87.

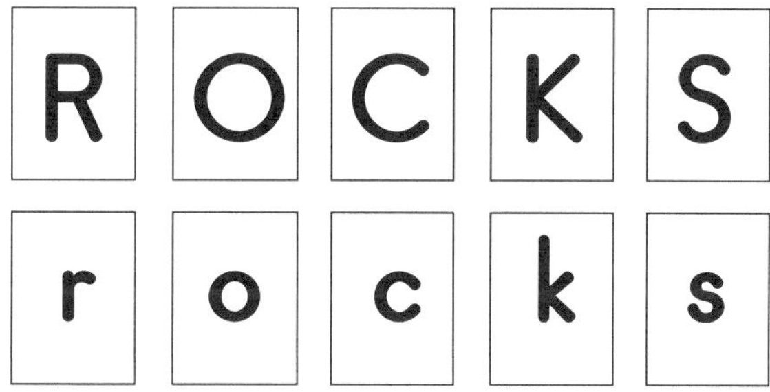

Beginning Readers

1. Use the poem that we created, to the right, and follow the process for rereading on Day 2 (page 82). A student copy of the poem is provided on page 88.
   - Have the students choral read and buddy read the poem.
   - Have the students reread the poem using different voices, such as a whispery voice or a happy voice.
   - Ask the students to dramatize the poem. Put them in groups and have them present their dramatizations.
2. Make copies of the poem for students (see page 89). Distribute one stanza to each student or pair of students. Have them cut apart the stanza into words or lines and then rebuild.
   - Extension: have each student or pair work on a different stanza.

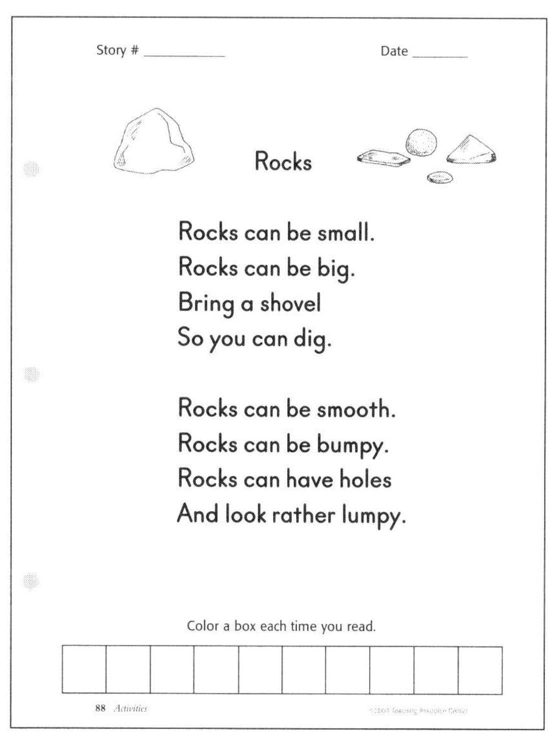
Story # ________ Date ______

Rocks

Rocks can be small.
Rocks can be big.
Bring a shovel
So you can dig.

Rocks can be smooth.
Rocks can be bumpy.
Rocks can have holes
And look rather lumpy.

Color a box each time you read.

88 Activities

3. Have the students use the pattern (Figure A) to create individual books or a class book. A student copy is provided on page 90.
4. Add a Readers Theatre script to the Personal Reader. Here are two scripts we created (Figures B and C). Student copies of the scripts are provided on pages 91 and 92.
5. Have the students hunt for words that begin with a certain letter or pattern that is developmentally appropriate. Beginning readers might hunt for:
   - known words
   - beginning and ending consonants
   - rhyming words
   - phonograms (word families)
   - blends and digraphs
   - short vowel CVC words
6. Have the students write what they now know about rocks (Figure D).

I see a rock on the ground .

Figure A

Story # ____________ Date ______

Ten Little Rocks

Reader 1: Ten little rocks rolling on the ground.
Reader 2: One rolled away and couldn't be found.
Reader 1: I called my sister and my sister groaned,
Reader 2: No more rocks rolling on the ground!

Color a box each time you read.

Figure B

Story # ____________ Date ______

I Found a Rock

Reader 1: I found a rock nice and flat.
Reader 2: Tell me what you did with that.
Reader 1: I skipped it on the water just so, but it just sunk way below.
Reader 2: Tell me what did you do then?
Reader 1: I found a rock by the trail and sat on it to rest a spell.
Reader 2: Tell me what did you do then?
Reader 1: I found a rock by my foot. I turned it over and took a look.
Reader 2: What did you see under that rock?
Reader 1: I saw bugs and worms and mud.
Reader 2: Sounds like rocks are really cool.
Reader 1: Yes, would you like to find rocks, too?

Figure C

Rocks come in different shapes and sizes.

Some rocks are heavier than others.

Chalk rocks can be used to draw on the street.

We can see rocks better with a magnifying glass.

Figure D

Story # __________ Date __________

Rocks

Rocks can be small.
Rocks can be big.
Bring a shovel
So you can dig.

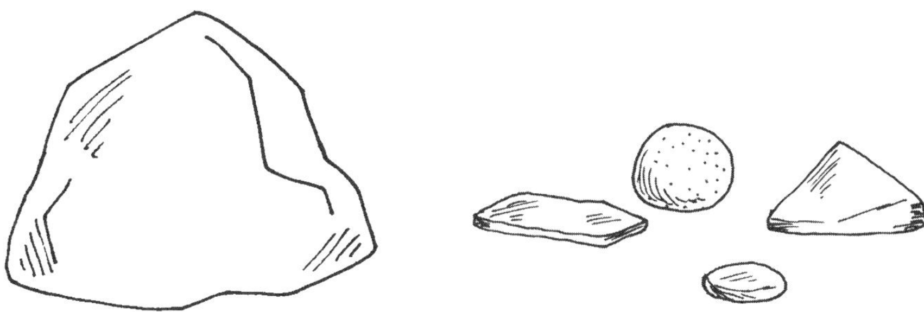

Color a box each time you read.

Rocks

Rocks can be small.

Rocks can be big.

Bring a shovel

So you can dig.

S
s
K
k
C
c
O
o
R
r

Story # ___________ Date ________

Rocks

Rocks can be small.
Rocks can be big.
Bring a shovel
So you can dig.

Rocks can be smooth.
Rocks can be bumpy.
Rocks can have holes
And look rather lumpy.

Color a box each time you read.

Rocks

Rocks can be small.

Rocks can be big.

Bring a shovel

So you can dig.

Rocks can be smooth.

Rocks can be bumpy.

Rocks can have holes

And look rather lumpy.

I see a rock ______________.

I see a rock ______________.

Story # ________________ Date ________

Ten Little Rocks

Reader 1: Ten little rocks rolling on the ground.

Reader 2: One rolled away and couldn't be found.

Reader 1: I called my sister and my sister groaned,

Reader 2: "No more rocks rolling on the ground!"

Color a box each time you read.

Story # ________________ Date ________

I Found a Rock

Reader 1: I found a rock nice and flat.

Reader 2: Tell me what you did with that.

Reader 1: I skipped it on the water just so, but it just sunk way below.

Reader 2: Tell me, what did you do then?

Reader 1: I found a rock by the trail and sat on it to rest a spell.

Reader 2: Tell me, what did you do then?

Reader 1: I found a rock by my foot. I turned it over and took a look.

Reader 2: What did you see under that rock?

Reader 1: I saw bugs and worms and mud.

Reader 2: Sounds like rocks are really cool.

Reader 1: Yes, would you like to find rocks, too?

Color a box each time you read.

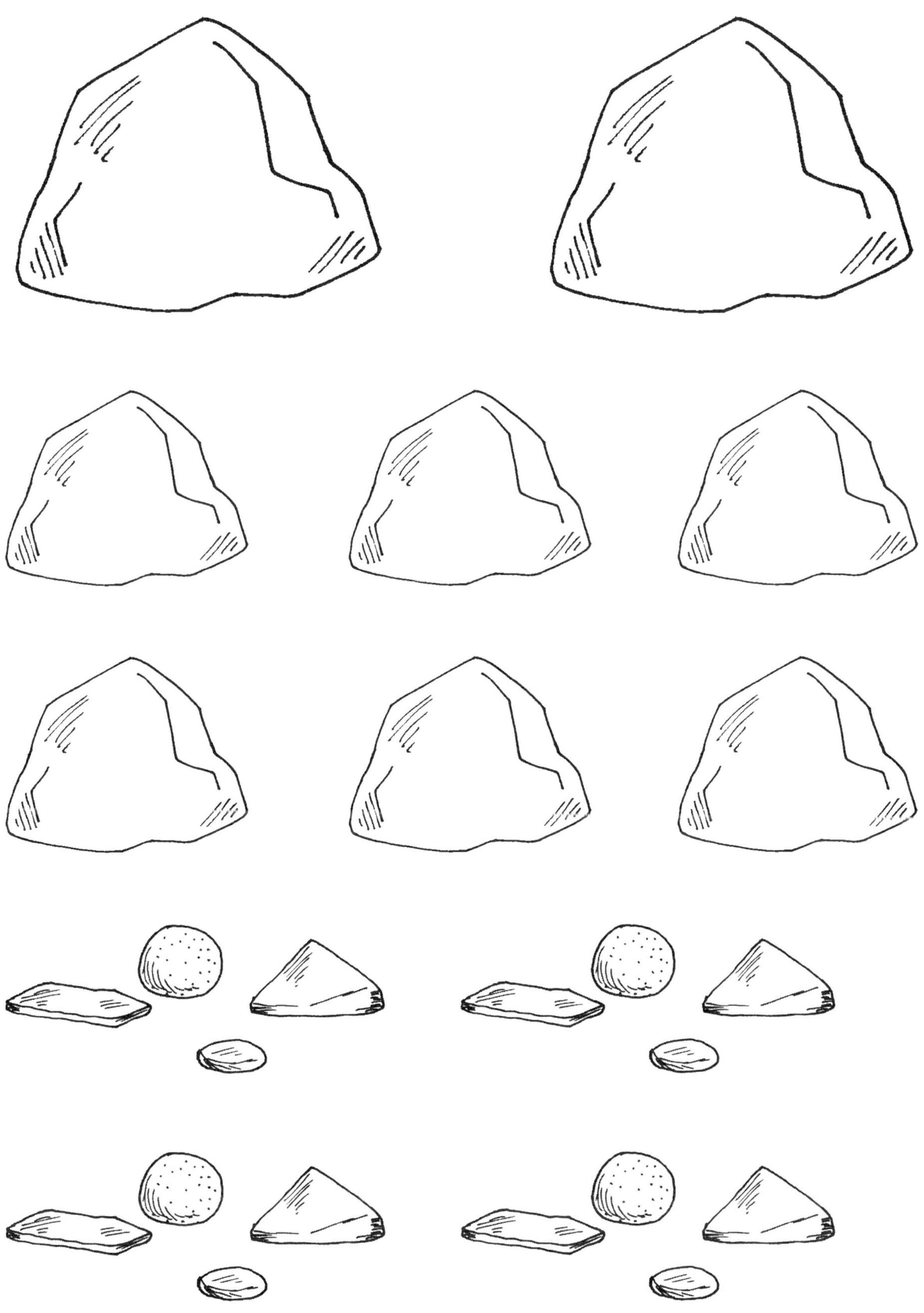

Activity 6
Flower Explorations

Materials

- One flower for each student
- Another flower for each student to place in a vase after the exploration
- Flower diagram enlarged and displayed for the small group
- Paper towels
- Cubes or paper clips for measuring
- Chart paper
- Student copies of rhyme (Emergent level, page 99) or poem (Beginning level, page 105)
- Copies of flower pictures (page 106–107, optional)

DAY 1

The Language Experience

Have the students dissect a flower and develop a dictation based on this experience and discussion. Teachers might want to use the simple terms *petal, leaf,* and *stem* with early beginning readers and the terms *stigma, stamen,* and *pistil* with late beginning readers.

- Pass one flower among the students. *"What do you notice about this flower? How does it smell? What colors do you see?"*
- Pass out a flower, a paper towel, and a magnifying glass to each student. *"Take off one petal at a time. Look at a petal under the magnifying glass. What do you see? How many petals do you have? How do the petals feel?"*
- Examine the inside of the flower. *"What does the inside look like under the magnifying glass? Touch the inside of the flower. What do you see on your fingers?"*
- Measure the stem with cubes or paper clips. *"Look at the stem under the magnifying glass. What do you see? Measure your stem. How many cubes/paper clips did you use?"*
- Have the students talk with a neighbor about what they learned. *"Tell your neighbor about your favorite part of looking at the flowers today."*

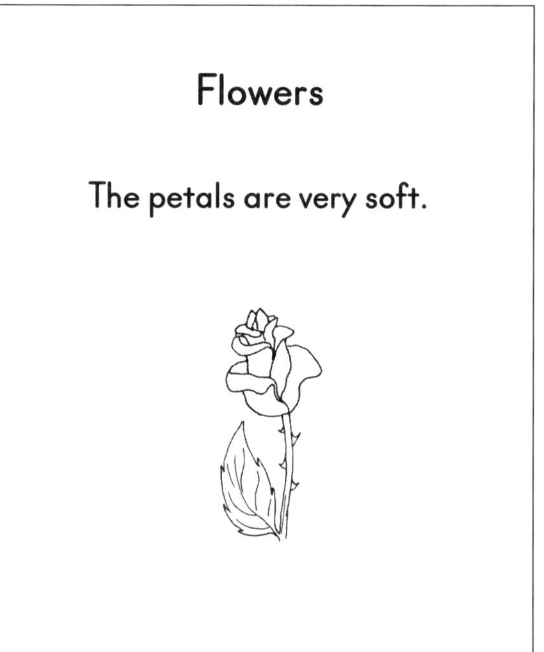

Emergent reader chart sample

Chart the Experience

Chart and Read: *Emergent Readers*

- Guide the small group in dictating a sentence about the experience. *"Let's write a sentence about the flowers on our chart. What is the most important thing to say about the flowers?"* Students often focus on color. Help them to form a one-sentence dictation. Say each word as you write it.

- Reread the sentence and ask the students for a title.
- Record the title.
- Point to words as students reread the chart.
- Choral read with the students while you point to the words.
- Choral read while a student points to the words.
- Draw a simple flower on the chart or use the reproducibles on pages 106 and 107.

Chart and Read: *Beginning Readers*

- Have a large sheet of chart paper ready for writing students' sentences. "Think about the sentence you want me to write on the chart." As each student dictates a sentence, write it on the chart and repeat the words.
- Use names and color-code the sentences to help support Beginning readers.
- Read the chart to the group.
- Ask the group to decide on a title. "Now we have our sentences. I will read the chart. While I am reading it, I'd like you to think about what would make a good title. Let's get some ideas and then decide which one to use." Record the title at the top of the chart.
- Choral read with the students while you point to the words.
- Choral read while a student points to the words.
- Draw a simple flower on the chart or use the reproducibles on pages 106 and 107.

Flowers

Gabino said, "I like the yellow flower."
Justin said, "My stem was long."
Baillie said, "My flower had fifteen petals."
Carrie said, "The red flowers smelled good."

Beginning reader chart sample

Instructions for making student copies of chart experience for rereading:

- Type the chart (using a 26- to 36-point font) and make copies for each student in the group.
- Be sure to leave an extra wide margin on the left side of the page for hole punching and space at the bottom of the page for a picture.
- Add: *Story* _____ on the upper left corner and *Date* _____ on the upper right corner.
- These typed charts will be used for rereading on subsequent days.

Chart and Read:
Middle/Late Beginning Readers

As students become more fluent readers, they will not need the support of color or names and will be able to reread paragraphs.

DAY 2
Rereading in the Personal Reader
Emergent and Beginning Readers

- Make a copy of the dictation for each student in the group. These typed Group Experience Charts will be used for rereading on subsequent days. (See page 94 for instructions.)
- Pass out the copies and have the students put them in their Personal Readers.
- Reread the chart to the group.
- Choral read while one or two students point to the words.
- Ask the students to point to and reread either their sentence or the whole chart.
- Have the students partner read the individual copies in their Personal Readers.
- Have them underline three or four known words on their copies and write the words at the bottom of the page.
- Have them draw a picture on their individual copies to help remember the text. For students who need additional support, have them draw a picture by each line.

DAYS 3–7
Extension Activities
Emergent Readers

Read aloud *Brown Bear, Brown Bear, What Do You See?* by Bill Martin Jr.

1. Use the rhyme (to the right), and follow the process for rereading on Day 2. Give each student a copy (provided on page 99) to use as a reference when they rebuild the rhyme line by line.
2. Act out the pattern or create a fingerplay.

Flowers

We looked at flowers. They smelled good. We took off the petals and looked inside the flower. We saw the pistils in the center. They were fuzzy and soft. We could see lines on the petals under the magnifying glass. Then we measured the stem with Unifix cubes. Some of the stems were long and some of them were short.

Then we filled a vase with water and took turns putting a flower in a vase. Each flower has a name on it so we can remember which flower belongs to us.

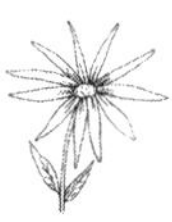

Middle/Late Beginning reader chart sample

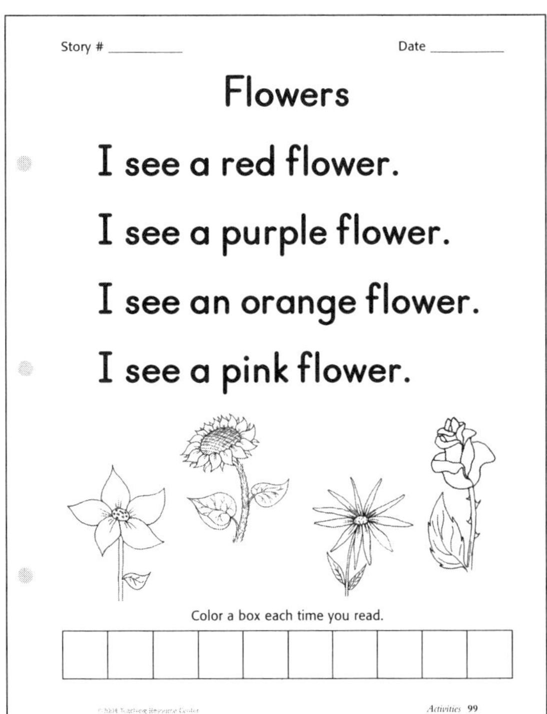

Story # ________ Date ________

Flowers

I see a red flower.

I see a purple flower.

I see an orange flower.

I see a pink flower.

Color a box each time you read.

Activities 99

3. Using the blacklines on page 100, have students arrange the lines in order by matching them to the chart.

Flowers

I see a red flower.

I see a purple flower.

I see an orange flower.

I see a pink flower.

4. Have the students hunt for particular letters on the chart. Use Wikki Stix or highlighter tape to identify the letters.
5. Have the students match uppercase letters to lowercase letters. A student copy is provided on page 101.

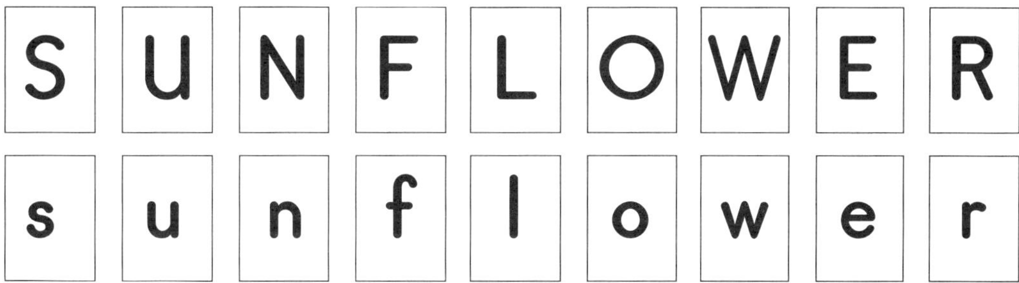

Beginning Readers

1. Read aloud *Brown Bear, Brown Bear, What Do You See?* by Bill Martin Jr. Use the poem (to the right), and follow the process for rereading on Day 2 (page 96). A student copy of the poem is provided on page 102.
2. Make copies of the poem for students (see page 103). Distribute one stanza to each student or pair of students. Have them cut apart the stanza into words or lines and then rebuild.

Story # ________ Date ________

Sunflower

Sunflower, sunflower

What do you see?

I see a bee visiting me!

Color a box each time you read.

102 Activities

Sunflower

Sunflower, sunflower

What do you see?

I see a bee visiting me!

3. This poem (Figure A) can be introduced to late beginning readers (sung to the tune of "If You're Happy and You Know It").
   - Students can draw large flowers and hold them up as they are singing the song. Some teachers like to use flower pointers for the students to use when rereading the chart.
4. After reading *Brown Bear, Brown Bear, What Do You See?* brainstorm a list of creatures that might be seen on a flower. This might include a butterfly, a caterpillar, an ant, a grasshopper, a worm, a bird, etc. Have the students use these words with the pattern (Figure B) to create individual books or a class book. A student copy is provided on page 104.
5. Have the students do a science experiment where they give color to white carnations by keeping the stems in colored water. Each student could then create an illustrated fact page about the experiment for a class book.
6. Have the students hunt for words that begin with a certain letter or pattern that is developmentally appropriate. Beginning readers might hunt for:
   - known words
   - beginning and ending consonants
   - rhyming words
   - phonograms (word families)
   - blends and digraphs
   - short vowel CVC words
7. Ask the students to write what they now know about flowers (Figure C).

Figure B

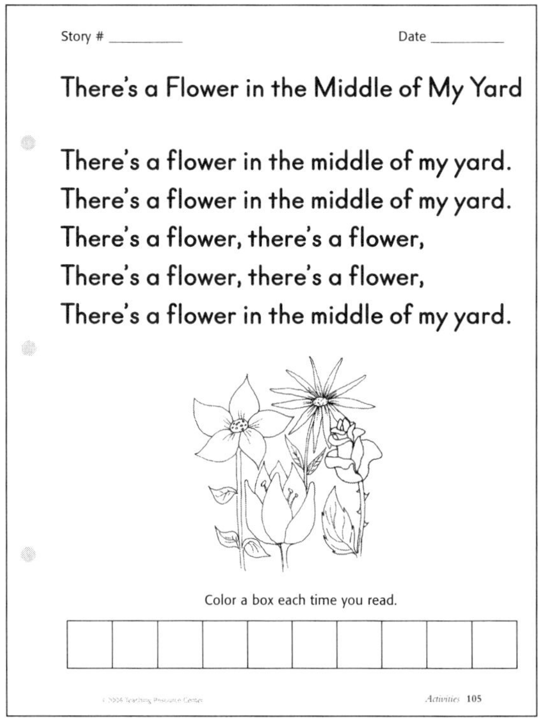

Story # ________ Date ________

There's a Flower in the Middle of My Yard

There's a flower in the middle of my yard.
There's a flower in the middle of my yard.
There's a flower, there's a flower,
There's a flower, there's a flower,
There's a flower in the middle of my yard.

Color a box each time you read.

Activities 105

Figure A

Flowers have green stems.
Flowers have soft petals.
Flowers need water.
Flowers smell good.

Figure C

Story # __________ Date __________

Flowers

I see a red flower.

I see a purple flower.

I see an orange flower.

I see a pink flower.

Color a box each time you read.

Flowers

I see a red flower.

I see a purple flower.

I see an orange flower.

I see a pink flower.

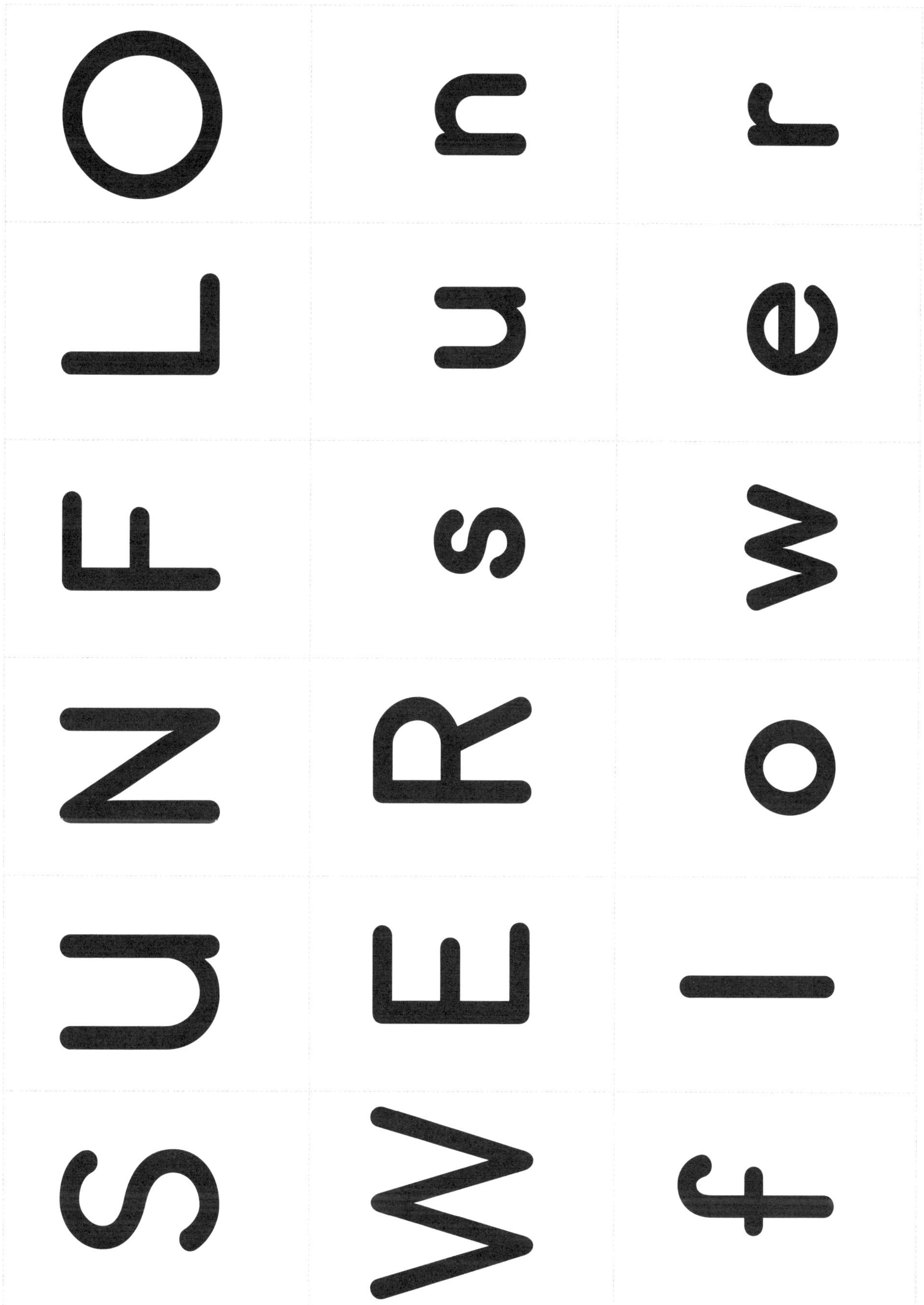
S
U
N
F
L
O
W
E
R
s
u
n
f
l
o
w
e
r

Story # __________ Date __________

Sunflower

Sunflower, sunflower
What do you see?
I see a bee visiting me!

Color a box each time you read.

Sunflower

Sunflower, sunflower

What do you see?

I see a bee visiting me!

Sunflower, sunflower
What do you see?
I see a ____________ visiting me.

Sunflower, sunflower
What do you see?
I see a ____________ visiting me.

Story # __________ Date __________

There's a Flower in the Middle of My Yard

There's a flower in the middle of my yard.
There's a flower in the middle of my yard.
There's a flower, there's a flower,
There's a flower, there's a flower,
There's a flower in the middle of my yard

Color a box each time

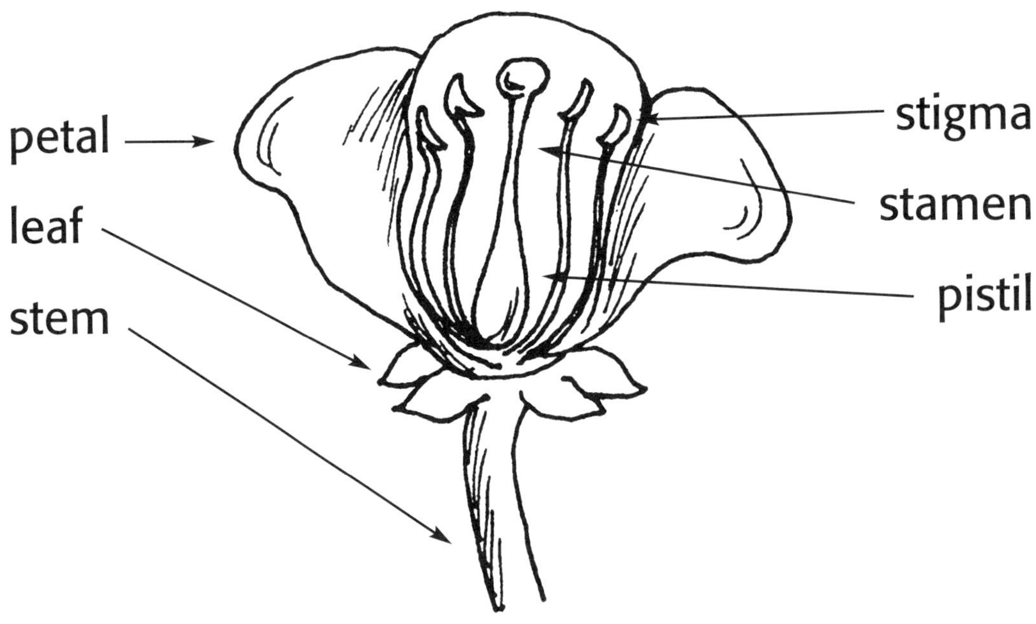
petal
leaf
stem
stigma
stamen
pistil

Activity 7
Chicken Soup With Rice

Materials

Utensils:

- Knife
- Cutting board
- Cooking pot
- Can opener
- Spoon
- Clear plastic glasses

Food:

- Carrots
- Onions
- Squash
- Cooked chicken
- Rice
- Chicken broth in cans

- Student copies of rhyme (Emergent level, page 112) or poem (Beginning level, page 115)
- Copies of soup bowl and pot pictures (page 119, optional)

DAY 1

The Language Experience

Begin by providing each student with a bowl of chicken soup with rice (or a vegetarian alternative) and developing a dictation based on this experience and discussion. Some teachers enjoy writing the dictation about making the soup.

- Pour the soup into clear plastic glasses and have the students look and smell. *"What do you notice about this soup? How does it smell? How does it look? What colors do you see?*
- Have the students taste the soup. *"How does the soup taste? How does the soup feel?"*
- Allow the students to talk to a neighbor about what they learned. *"Think of three things to say about the soup."*

Chart the Experience

Chart and Read: *Emergent Readers*

- Guide the small group in dictating a sentence about the experience. *"Let's write a sentence about the soup on our chart. What is the most important thing to say about the soup?"* Help them to form a one-sentence dictation. Say each word as you write it.
- Reread the sentence and ask the students for a title.
- Record the title.
- Point to words as students reread the chart.
- Choral read with the students while you point to the words.
- Choral read while a student points to the words.
- Draw a bowl of soup on the chart or use the reproducible on page 119.

Chicken Soup with Rice

We like to eat soup.

Emergent reader chart sample

Chart and Read:
Beginning Readers

- Have a large sheet of chart paper ready for writing students' sentences. *"Think about the sentence you want me to write on the chart."* As each student dictates a sentence, write it on the chart and repeat the words.
- Use names and color-code the sentences to help support Beginning readers.
- Read the chart to the group.
- Ask the group to decide on a title. *"Now we have our sentences. I will read the chart. While I am reading it, I'd like you to think about what would make a good title. Let's get some ideas and then decide which one to use."* Record the title at the top of the chart.
- Choral read with the students while you point to the words.
- Choral read while a student points to the words.
- Draw a simple pot of soup on the chart or use the reproducible on page 119.

Soup

Jasmine said, "It was full of rice."

Robert said, "I liked the way it tasted."

Davina said, "It was a pretty yellow ."

Matt said, "It should have had more rice."

Lalita said, "I like soup!"

Beginning reader chart sample

Instructions for making student copies of chart experience for rereading:

- Type the chart (using a 26- to 36-point font) and make copies for each student in the group.
- Be sure to leave an extra wide margin on the left side of the page for hole punching and space at the bottom of the page for a picture.
- Add: *Story* _____ on the upper left corner and *Date* _____ on the upper right corner.
- These typed charts will be used for rereading on subsequent days.

Chart and Read:
Middle/Late Beginning Readers

As students become more fluent readers, they will not need the support of color or names and will be able to reread paragraphs.

Chicken Soup with Rice

We ate chicken soup today. It was made with chicken broth and rice. It was a pretty yellow color. The rice was soft and white. You could not see through the soup if you looked at it in the light.

Tomorrow we are going to make chicken soup with rice. We will need to bring carrots, onions, chicken, rice, chicken broth, squash, pepper, salt, and onions. We will need to cook it all day in the crock pot.

Middle/Late Beginning reader chart sample

DAY 2

Rereading in the Personal Reader

Emergent and Beginning Readers

- Make a copy of the dictation for each student in the group. These typed Group Experience Charts will be used for rereading on subsequent days. (See page 108 for instructions.)
- Pass out the copies and have the students put them in their Personal Readers.
- Reread the chart to the group.
- Choral read while one or two students point to the words.
- Ask the students to point to and reread either their sentence or the whole chart.
- Have the students partner read the individual copies in their Personal Readers.
- Have them underline three or four known words on their copies and write the words at the bottom of the page.
- Have them draw a picture on their individual copies to help remember the text. For students who need additional support, have them draw a picture by each line.

DAYS 3–7

Extension Activities

Emergent Readers

1. Use the rhyme (to the right), and follow the process for rereading on Day 2. Give each student a copy (provided on page 112) to use as a reference when they rebuild the rhyme line by line.
2. Act out the rhyme or create a fingerplay.
3. Using the blacklines on page 113, have students arrange the lines in order by matching them to the chart.

Story # ________ Date ________

Soup

Soup, soup

Soup is yummy!

Soup, soup

Soup in my tummy.

Color a box each time you read.

112 *Activities*

Soup
Soup, soup
Soup is yummy!
Soup, soup
Soup in my tummy.

4. Have the students hunt for particular letters on the chart. Use Wikki Stix or highlighter tape to identify the letters.
5. Have the students match uppercase letters to lowercase letters. A student copy of the letters is provided on page 114.

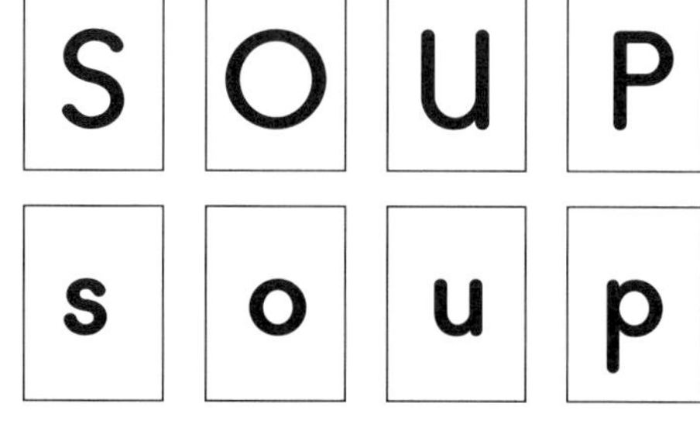

Beginning Readers

1. Use the poem that we created, to the right, and follow the process for rereading on Day 2 (page 110). A student copy of the poem is provided on page 115.
   - Have the students choral read and buddy read the poem.
   - Have the students reread the poem using different voices, such as a whispery voice or a happy voice.
   - Ask the students to dramatize the poem. Put them in groups and have them present their dramatizations.
2. Make copies of the poem for students. Distribute one stanza to each student or pair of students. Have them cut apart the stanza into words or lines and then rebuild.
   - Extension: have each student or pair work on a different stanza.
3. Have the students use the pattern about soup (Figure B) to create individual books or a class book. A student copy is provided on page 117.
4. Add a Readers Theatre script to the Personal Reader. Here is a script we created (Figure C). A student copy of the script is provided on page 118.
5. Have the students hunt for words that begin with a certain letter or pattern that is developmentally appropriate. Beginning readers might hunt for:
   - known words
   - beginning and ending consonants
   - rhyming words
   - phonograms (word families)
   - blends and digraphs
   - short vowel CVC words
6. Have the students write what they now know about making soup (see Figure D).

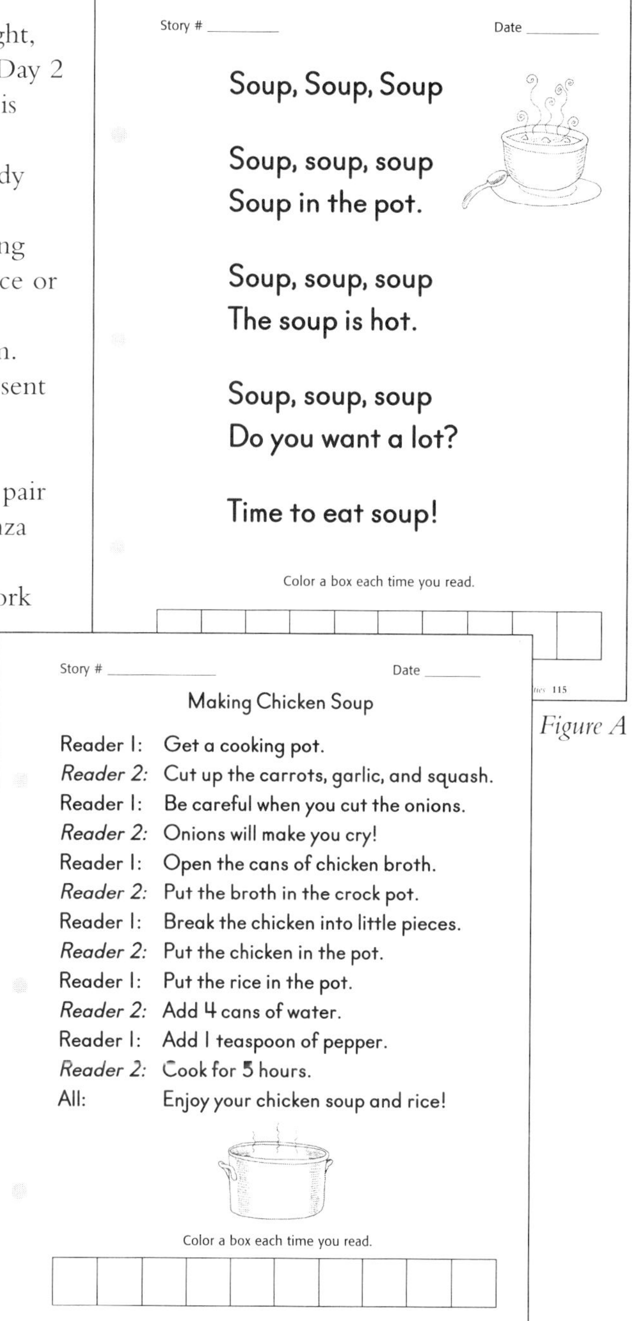

Story # ________ Date ________

Soup, Soup, Soup

Soup, soup, soup
Soup in the pot.

Soup, soup, soup
The soup is hot.

Soup, soup, soup
Do you want a lot?

Time to eat soup!

Color a box each time you read.

Figure A

Story # ________ Date ________

Making Chicken Soup

Reader 1:	Get a cooking pot.
Reader 2:	Cut up the carrots, garlic, and squash.
Reader 1:	Be careful when you cut the onions.
Reader 2:	Onions will make you cry!
Reader 1:	Open the cans of chicken broth.
Reader 2:	Put the broth in the crock pot.
Reader 1:	Break the chicken into little pieces.
Reader 2:	Put the chicken in the pot.
Reader 1:	Put the rice in the pot.
Reader 2:	Add 4 cans of water.
Reader 1:	Add 1 teaspoon of pepper.
Reader 2:	Cook for 5 hours.
All:	Enjoy your chicken soup and rice!

Color a box each time you read.

118 Activities

Figure C

Put __rice__ **in the soup pot.**

Figure B

Soup is easy to make.

Soup can have different vegetables in it.

Soup takes a long time to cook.

Soup can have pasta or rice added to it.

Figure D

Story # __________ Date __________

Soup

Soup, soup
Soup is yummy!
Soup, soup
Soup in my tummy.

Color a box each time you read.

Soup

Soup, soup

Soup is yummy!

Soup, soup

Soup in my tummy.

S	O	U	P
s	o	u	p

Story # ___________ Date ___________

Soup, Soup, Soup

Soup, soup, soup
Soup in the pot.

Soup, soup, soup
The soup is hot.

Soup, soup, soup
Do you want a lot?

Time to eat soup!

Color a box each time you read.

Soup, Soup, Soup

Soup, soup, soup

Soup in the pot.

Soup, soup, soup

The soup is hot.

Soup, soup, soup

Do you want a lot?

Time to eat soup!

Put ____________ in the soup pot.

Put ____________ in the soup pot.

Story # ________________ Date ________

Making Chicken Soup

Reader 1: Get a cooking pot.
Reader 2: Cut up the carrots, garlic, and squash.
Reader 1: Be careful when you cut the onions.
Reader 2: Onions will make you cry!
Reader 1: Open the cans of chicken broth.
Reader 2: Put the broth in the crock pot.
Reader 1: Break the chicken into little pieces.
Reader 2: Put the chicken in the pot.
Reader 1: Put the rice in the pot.
Reader 2: Add 4 cans of water.
Reader 1: Add 1 teaspoon of pepper.
Reader 2: Cook for 5 hours.
All: Enjoy your chicken soup and rice!

Color a box each time you read.

Activity 8
Magnet Explorations

Materials

- Magnetic wands or other magnets
- Items that magnets will attract: paper clips, screws, keys, forks, and spoons
- Items that magnets will not attract: paper, wooden blocks, erasers, material swatches, pencils, etc.
- Soda cans
- One container for each student's item collection
- Student copies of rhyme (Emergent level, page 125) or poem (Beginning level, page 128)
- Copies of magnet pictures (page 132, optional)
- **Warning: Be sure to tell your students to keep all magnets away from the computer area!**

DAY 1

The Language Experience

- Have students share what they know about magnets. *"Today we are going to work with magnets. Where have you seen magnets? What do you know about magnets?"*
- Demonstrate the ability of a magnet to pull a paper clip through the air by placing a paper clip flat on the table a few inches from the magnet. *"Try to pull a paper clip through the air with your magnet. What happens if you put the paper clip farther away from the magnet?"*
- Demonstrate that magnets will not attract a soda can. *"Try to make your magnet stick to the soda can. What happens? Why do you think the magnet will stick to a paper clip but not to a soda can?"*
- Provide each student with a tray of metal and non-metal items. *"Which items in your tray stick to the magnet? Which items will not stick to the magnet? What do the objects that stick to the magnet? What do the objects that stick to the magnets have in common?"*
- Demonstrate the ability of magnetic poles to students. *"Pick up two magnets from your tray. Put them end to end. What happens? What happens if you turn the ends around?"*
- For students in the late beginning stage, expand the magnet exploration to include vocabulary words: *attract*, *repel*, *poles*, etc.

Chart the Experience

Chart and Read: *Emergent Readers*

- Guide the small group in dictating a sentence

Magnets

Magnets stick to paper clips.

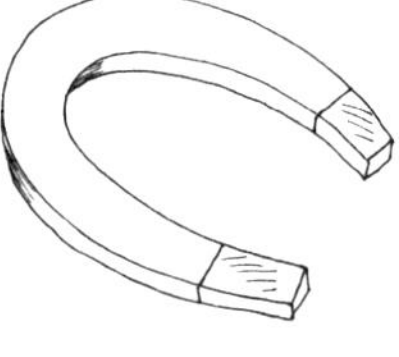

Emergent reader chart sample

about the experience. *"Let's write a sentence about the magnets on our chart. What is the most important thing to say about the magnets?"* Help them to form a one-sentence dictation. Say each word as you write it.

- Reread the sentence and ask the students for a title.
- Record the title.
- Point to words as students reread the chart.
- Choral read with the students while you point to the words.
- Choral read while a student points to the words.
- Draw a simple magnet on the chart or use the reproducible on page 132.

Chart and Read: *Beginning Readers*

- Have a large sheet of chart paper ready for writing students' sentences. "Think about the sentence you want me to write on the chart." As each student dictates a sentence, write it on the chart and repeat the words.
- Use names and color-code the sentences to help support Beginning readers.
- Read the chart to the group.
- Ask the group to decide on a title. "Now we have our sentences. I will read the chart. While I am reading it, I'd like you to think about what would make a good title. Let's get some ideas and then decide which one to use." Record the title at the top of the chart.
- Choral read with the students while you point to the words.
- Choral read while a student points to the words.
- Draw a simple magnet on the chart or use the reproducible on page on 132.

Magnets

Chad said, "My magnet didn't stick to the wood."

Christina said, "The magnet pulled the paper clip across the table."

Hannah said, "The magnet picked up a bunch of paper clips."

Jake said, "The magnet would not pick up the paper or the pencil."

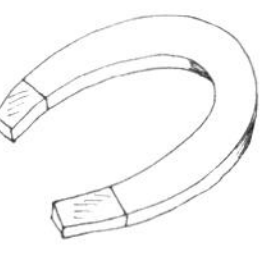

Beginning reader chart sample

Instructions for making student copies of chart experience for rereading:

- Type the chart (using a 26- to 36-point font) and make copies for each student in the group.
- Be sure to leave an extra wide margin on the left side of the page for hole punching and space at the bottom of the page for a picture.
- Add: *Story* _____ on the upper left corner and *Date* _____ on the upper right corner.
- These typed charts will be used for rereading on subsequent days.

Chart and Read:
Middle/Late Beginning Readers
As students become more fluent readers, they will not need the support of color or names and will be able to reread paragraphs.

Magnets

Today we played with magnets. All of the metal things stuck to the magnet. The magnet attracted spoons, forks and paper clips. It would not attract the material, wood or paper.

We also pulled a paper clip through the air with the strong magnet. When we stuck two magnets together we could feel the pull. We were surprised that the magnet would not stick to the soda can.

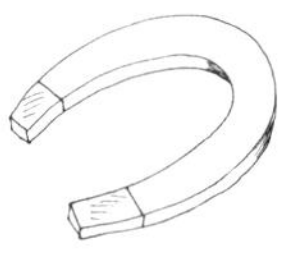

Middle/Late Beginning reader chart sample

DAY 2
Rereading in the Personal Reader
Emergent and Beginning Readers
- Make a copy of the dictation for each student in the group. These typed Group Experience Charts will be used for rereading on subsequent days. (See page 120 for instructions.)
- Pass out the copies and have the students put them in their Personal Readers.
- Reread the chart to the group.
- Choral read while one or two students point to the words.
- Ask the students to point to and reread either their sentence or the whole chart.
- Have the students partner read the individual copies in their Personal Readers.
- Have them underline three or four known words on their copies and write the words at the bottom of the page.
- Have them draw a picture on their individual copies to help remember the text. For students who need additional support, have them draw a picture by each line.

DAYS 3–7
Extension Activities
Emergent Readers
1. Use the rhyme (to the right), and follow the process for rereading on Day 2. Give each student a copy (provided on page 125) to use as a reference when they rebuild the rhyme line by line.
2. Act out the rhyme or create a fingerplay.

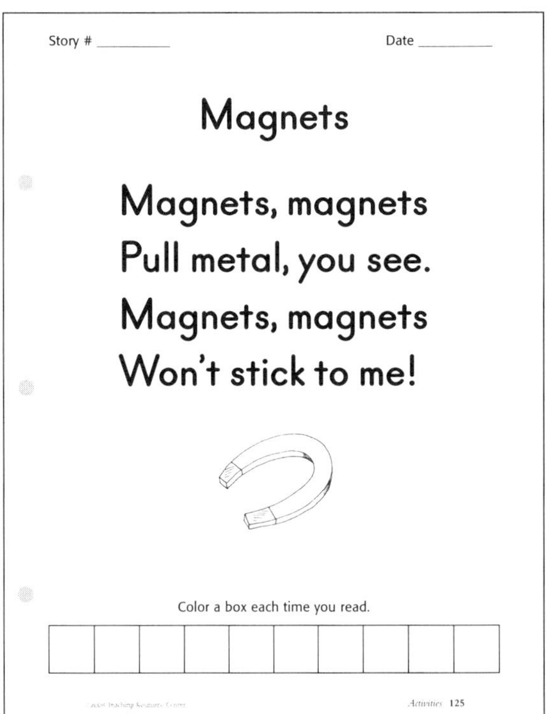

Story # ________ Date ________

Magnets

Magnets, magnets
Pull metal, you see.
Magnets, magnets
Won't stick to me!

Color a box each time you read.

Activities 125

3. Using the blacklines on page 126, have students arrange the lines in order by matching them to the chart.

Magnets

Magnets, magnets

Pull metal, you see.

Magnets, magnets

Won't stick to me!

4. Have the students hunt for particular letters on the chart. Use Wikki Stix or highlighter tape to identify them.
5. Have the students match uppercase letters to lowercase letters. A student copy is provided on page 127.

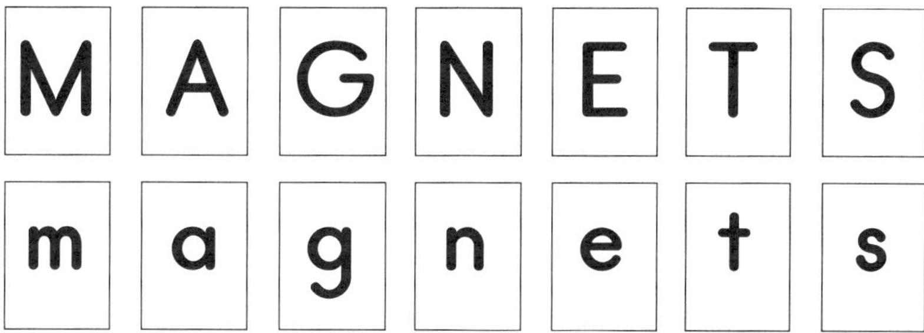

Beginning Readers

1. Use the poem that we created, to the right, and follow the process for rereading on Day 2 (page 122). A student copy of the poem is provided on page 128.
   - Have the students choral read and buddy read the poem.
   - Have the students reread the poem using different voices such as a whispery voice or a happy voice.
   - Ask the students to dramatize the poem. Put them in groups and have them present their dramatizations.
2. Make copies of the poem for students (see page 129). Distribute one stanza to each student or pair of students. Have them cut apart the stanza into words or lines and then rebuild.
   - Extension: have each student or pair work on a different stanza.

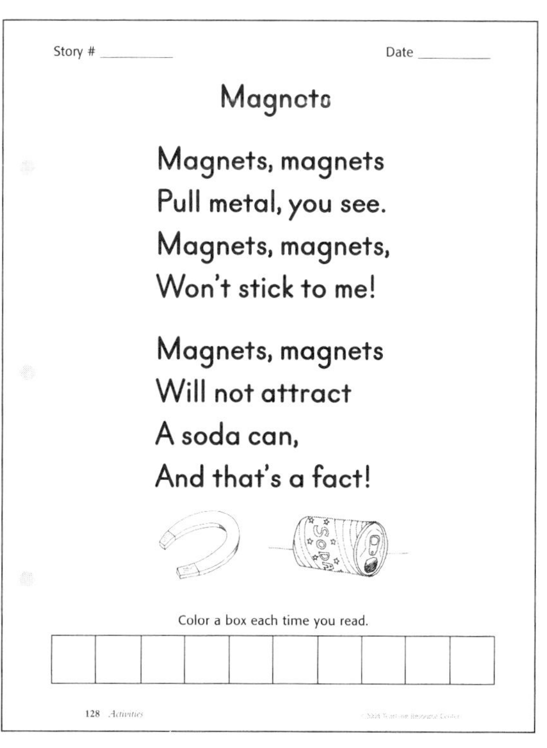

Story # ________ Date ________

Magnets

Magnets, magnets
Pull metal, you see.
Magnets, magnets,
Won't stick to me!

Magnets, magnets
Will not attract
A soda can,
And that's a fact!

Color a box each time you read.

3. Have the students use their knowledge of magnets to create their own flip book. A student copy is provided on page 130.
4. Read aloud *The Very Hungry Caterpillar* by Eric Carle. Add a Readers Theatre script to the Personal Reader. Here is one we created (Figure B). A student copy of the script is provided on page 131.
5. Have the students hunt for words that begin with a certain letter or pattern that is developmentally appropriate. Beginning readers might hunt for:
   - known words
   - beginning and ending consonants
   - rhyming words
   - phonograms (word families)
   - blends and digraphs
   - short vowel CVC words
6. Have the students write what they now know about magnets.

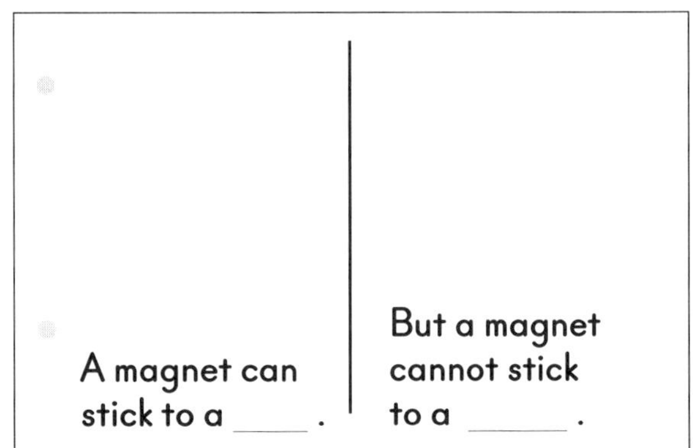

Figure A

Story # ____________ Date _______

The Very Sticky Magnet

Reader 1: On Monday, the very sticky magnet caught one paper clip.

Reader 2: On Tuesday, the very sticky magnet caught two keys.

Reader 3: On Wednesday, the very sticky magnet caught three nails.

Reader 4: On Thursday, the very sticky magnet caught four screws.

Reader 5: On Friday, the very sticky magnet caught five forks.

Reader 6: On Saturday, the very sticky magnet caught six spoons.

Reader 7: On Sunday, the very sticky magnet caught seven magnet friends.

Color a box each time you read.

Activities 131

Figure B

Magnets stick to metal.
Magnets won't stick to paper.
Magnets won't stick to a soda can.
A magnet can pull a paper clip to it.

Figure C

Story # __________ Date __________

Magnets

Magnets, magnets
Pull metal, you see.
Magnets, magnets
Won't stick to me!

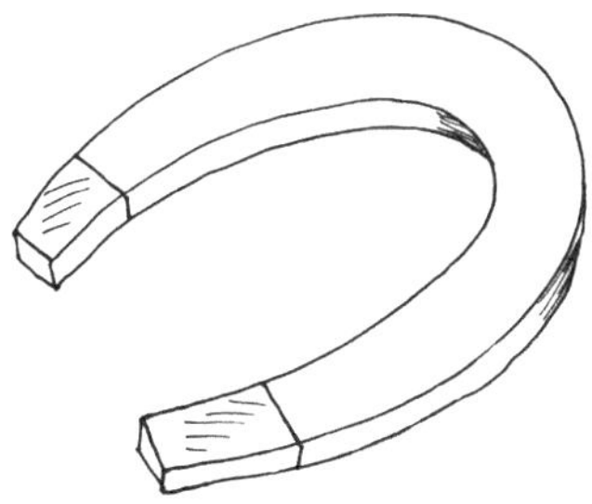

Color a box each time you read.

Magnets

Magnets, magnets

Pull metal, you see.

Magnets, magnets

Won't stick to me!

M	A	G	N
E	T	S	
m	a	g	n
e	t	s	

Story # __________ Date __________

Magnets

Magnets, magnets
Pull metal, you see.
Magnets, magnets,
Won't stick to me!

Magnets, magnets
Will not attract
A soda can,
And that's a fact!

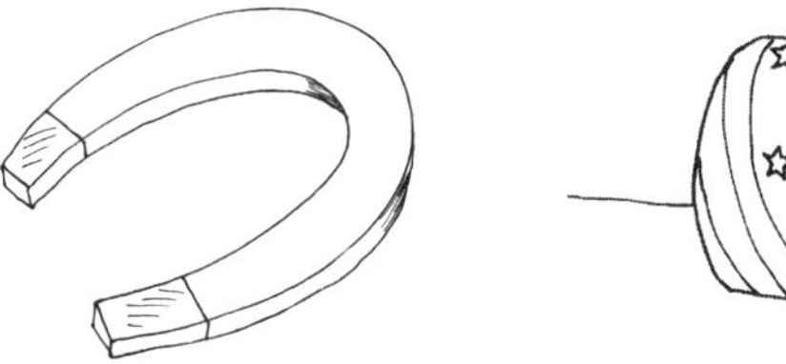

Color a box each time you read.

Magnets

Magnets, magnets
Pull metal, you see.
Magnets, magnets,
Won't stick to me!
Magnets, magnets
Will not attract
A soda can,
And that's a fact!

A magnet can stick to a ________.

But a magnet cannot stick to a ________.

A magnet can stick to a ________.

But a magnet cannot stick to a ________.

Story # ________________ Date ________

The Very Sticky Magnet

Reader 1: On Monday, the very sticky magnet caught one paper clip.

Reader 2: On Tuesday, the very sticky magnet caught two keys.

Reader 3: On Wednesday, the very sticky magnet caught three nails.

Reader 4: On Thursday, the very sticky magnet caught four screws.

Reader 5: On Friday, the very sticky magnet caught five forks.

Reader 6: On Saturday, the very sticky magnet caught six spoons.

Reader 7: On Sunday, the very sticky magnet caught seven magnet friends.

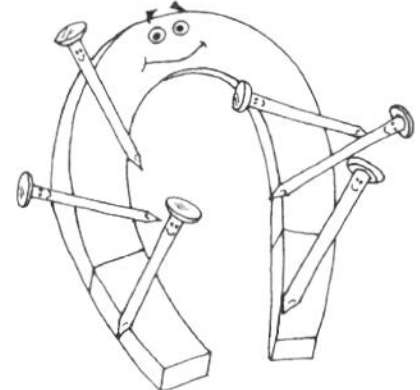

Color a box each time you read.

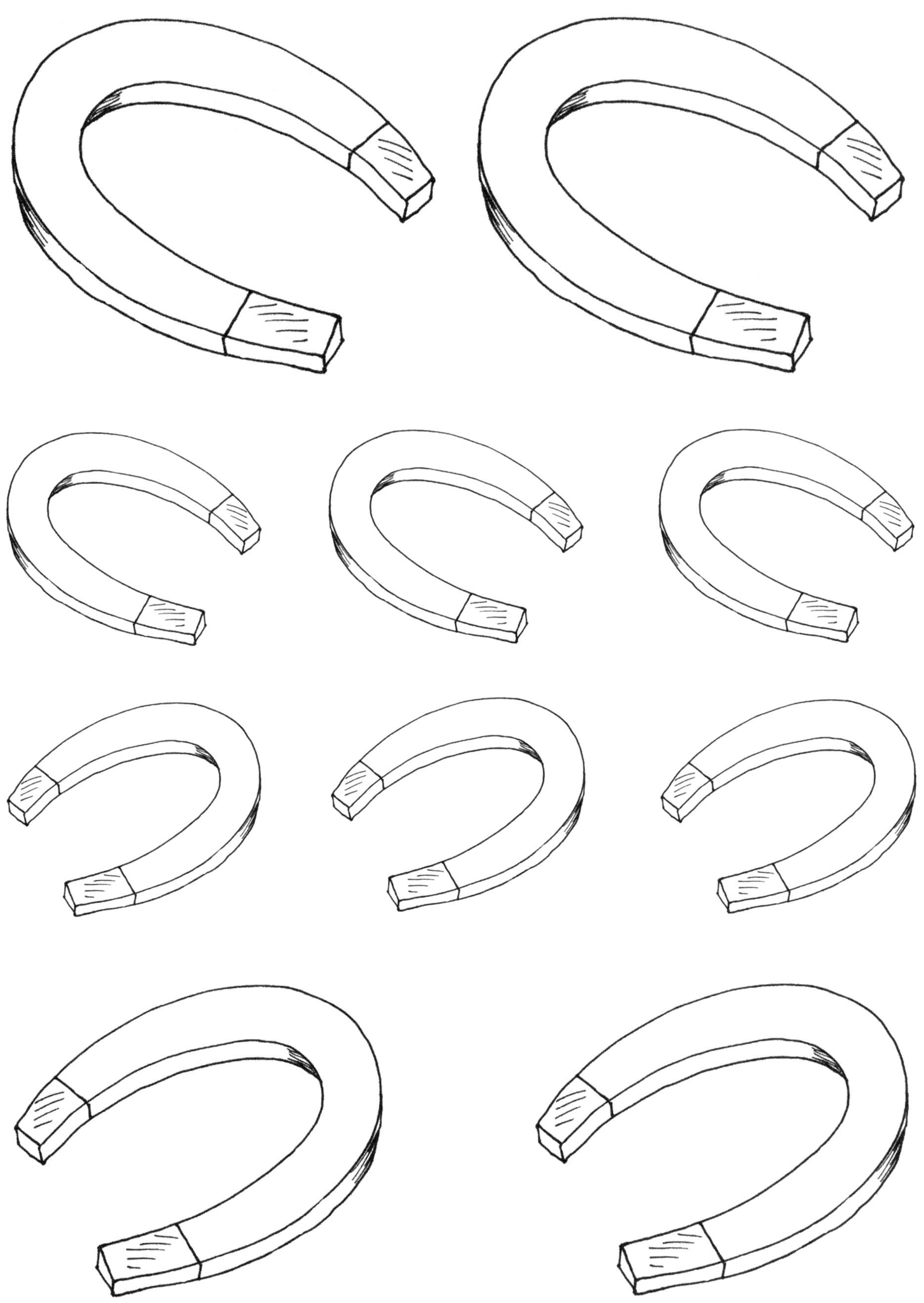

Activity 9
WORM RACES

Materials

- Earthworms (can be purchased at pet stores or stores that sell fishing equipment)
- Paper towels
- Magnifying glasses
- Rulers, cubes, or paper clips to measure
- Yarn or string
- Student copies of rhyme (Emergent level, page 138) or poem (Beginning level, page 141)
- Copies of worm pictures (page 144, optional)

The Language Experience

In this activity students examine earthworms. *Please note: It is important for students to handle worms with damp hands that have been washed and thoroughly rinsed. Soap and dry hands can be harmful to worms.* For those students who do not feel comfortable handling a worm can observe a neighbor's worm.

- Place one earthworm on a damp paper towel in front of the small group. *"Notice how carefully I placed the worm on the paper towel, so it won't be hurt while I observe it. What do you notice about this worm?"*
- Pass a damp paper towel with a worm on it and a magnifying glass to each student. *"Look carefully at the worm under the magnifying glass. Try to find the long red muscle on the underside of the worm. How does the worm move?"*
- Show students the rings on the worm in front of the small group. *"What do the rings of your worm look like under the magnifying glass?*
- Have the students work with a neighbor to find the head of the worm and to assist each other in measuring the worm. *"Look closely to find the worm's mouth. How can you tell which end is the mouth? Hold the worm for your neighbor while he or she measures it. About how many inches (or centimeters, cubes, or paper clips) long is your worm?"*
- If time permits, students can race their worms across a damp area of the floor. Yarn can be taped to the floor to create a start and finish line. *"Place your worms head to head at the start line. When I say go, let your worm wiggle to the finish line. I will watch for first, second, and third place winners."*

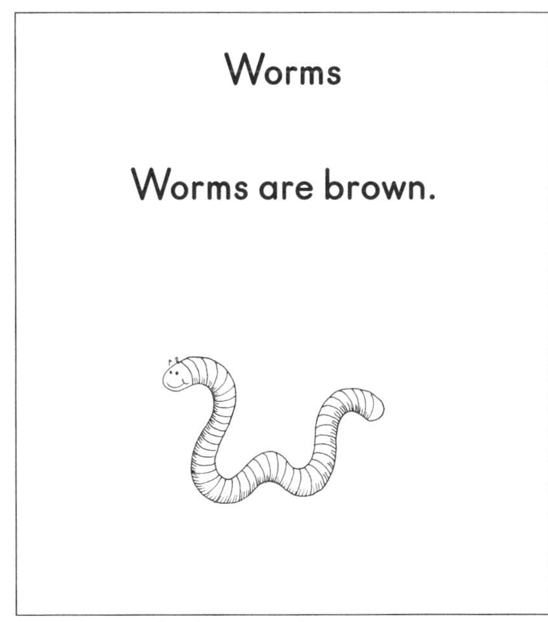

Emergent reader chart sample

Chart the Experience

Chart and Read: *Emergent Readers*

- Guide the small group in dictating a sentence about the experience. *"Let's write a sentence about worms on our chart. What is the most important thing to say about worms?"* Help them to form a one-sentence dictation. Say each word as you write it.

- Reread the sentence and ask the students for a title.
- Record the title.
- Point to words as students reread the chart.
- Choral read with the students while you point to the words.
- Choral read while a student points to the words.
- Draw a simple worm on the chart or use the reproducible on page 144.

Chart and Read: *Beginning Readers*

- Have a large sheet of chart paper ready for writing students' sentences. *"Think about the sentence you want me to write on the chart."* As each student dictates a sentence, write it on the chart and repeat the words.
- Use names and color-code the sentences to help support Beginning readers.
- Read the chart to the group.
- Ask the group to decide on a title. *"Now we have our sentences. I will read the chart. While I am reading it, I'd like you to think about what would make a good title. Let's get some ideas and then decide which one to use."* Record the title at the top of the chart.
- Choral read with the students while you point to the words.
- Choral read while a student points to the words.
- Draw a simple worm on the chart or use the reproducible on page on 144.

Worms

David said, "My worm came in second."

Selina said, "My worm was the longest one."

Sierra said, "I saw all the rings up close."

Mason said, "My worm was brown and wet."

Kristina said, "My worm came in last."

Beginning reader chart sample

Instructions for making student copies of chart experience for rereading:

- Type the chart (using a 26- to 36-point font) and make copies for each student in the group.
- Be sure to leave an extra wide margin on the left side of the page for hole punching and space at the bottom of the page for a picture.
- Add: *Story* _____ on the upper left corner and *Date* _____ on the upper right corner.
- These typed charts will be used for rereading on subsequent days.

Chart and Read:
Middle/Late Beginning Readers

As students become more fluent readers, they will not need the support of color or names and will be able to reread paragraphs.

Worms

Today we learned about worms. They were brown and wet. Some of us didn't want to touch them at first. We saw their rings under a magnifying glass. We also saw a long red muscle that went down the whole body of the worm. They moved fast. It was hard to tell which end was the head. After we looked at them, we helped each other measure them with Unifix cubes.

Next, we had a worm race. We had to watch our worms while they wiggled to the finish line. Some of the worms went sideways instead of straight. Only two of the worms made it across the finish line.

Middle/Late Beginning reader chart sample

DAY 2

Rereading in the Personal Reader

Emergent and Beginning Readers

- Make a copy of the dictation for each student in the group. These typed Group Experience Charts will be used for rereading on subsequent days. (See page 133 for instructions.)
- Pass out the copies and have the students put them in their Personal Readers.
- Reread the chart to the group.
- Choral read while one or two students point to the words.
- Ask the students to point to and reread either their sentence or the whole chart.
- Have the students partner read the individual copies in their Personal Readers.
- Have them underline three or four known words on their copies and write the words at the bottom of the page.
- Have them draw a picture on their individual copies to help remember the text. For students who need additional support, have them draw a picture by each line.

DAYS 3–7

Extension Activities

Emergent Readers

1. Use the rhyme (to the right), and follow the process for rereading on Day 2. Give each student a copy (provided on page 138) to use as a reference when they rebuild the rhyme line by line.
2. Act out the rhyme or create a fingerplay.

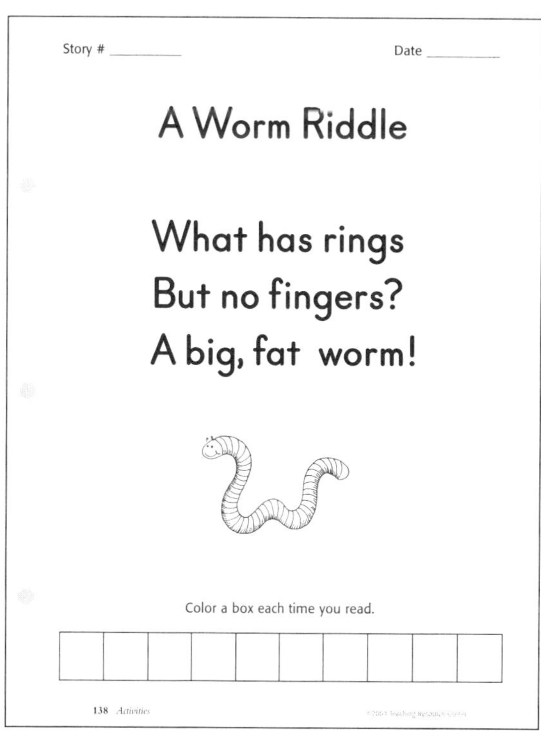

Story # ________ Date ________

A Worm Riddle

What has rings
But no fingers?
A big, fat worm!

Color a box each time you read.

138 Activities

3. Using the blacklines on page 139, have students arrange the lines in order by matching them to the chart.

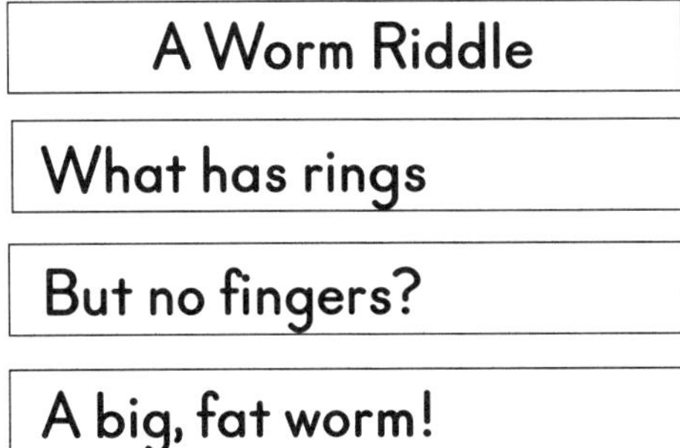

4. Have the students hunt for particular letters on the chart. Use Wikki Stix or highlighter tape to identify them.
5. Have the students match uppercase letters to lowercase letters. A student copy is provided on page 140.

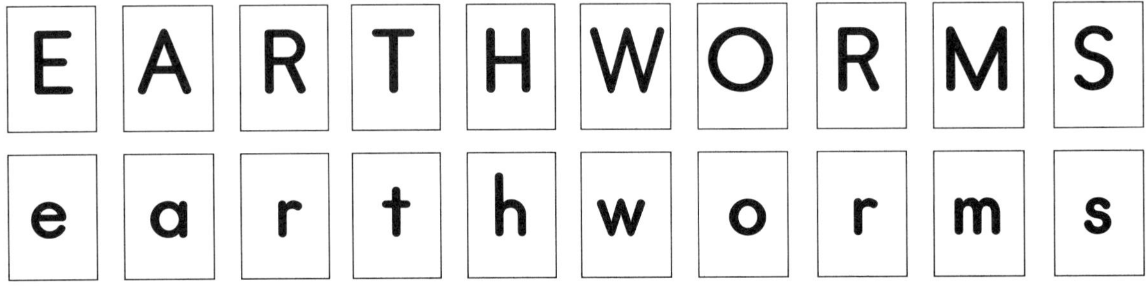

Beginning Readers

1. Use the poem (to the right), and follow the process for rereading on Day 2 (page 135). A student copy of the poem is provided on page 141.
   - Have the students choral read and buddy read the poem.
   - Have the students reread the poem using different voices such as a whispery voice or a happy voice.
   - Ask the students to dramatize the poem. Put them in groups and have them present their dramatizations.
2. Make copies of the poem for students (see page 142). Distribute one stanza to each student or pair of students. Have them cut apart the stanza into words or lines and then rebuild.
   - Extension: have each student or pair work on a different stanza.

Story # ________ Date ________

Nobody Likes Me

Nobody likes me.
Everybody hates me.
Guess I'll go eat worms.

Long, thin, slimy ones
Short, fat, juicy ones
Itsy, bitsy, fuzzy, wuzzy worms

Color a box each time you read.

Activities 141

3. Add a Readers Theatre script to the Personal Reader. Here is one we created for partners to read. A student copy of the script is provided on page 143.
4. Have the students hunt for words that begin with a certain letter or pattern that is developmentally appropriate. Beginning readers might hunt for:
   - known words
   - beginning and ending consonants
   - rhyming words
   - phonograms (word families)
   - blends and digraphs
   - short vowel CVC words
5. Have the students write what they now know about worms.
6. Bring in candy worms and let the students
   - write stories about candy worms.
   - make cupcakes in flower pots with candy worms.
   - make pudding in flower pots with Oreo cookie crumbs on the top and candy worms inside.
   - glue the candy worms on construction paper and write poems about them.

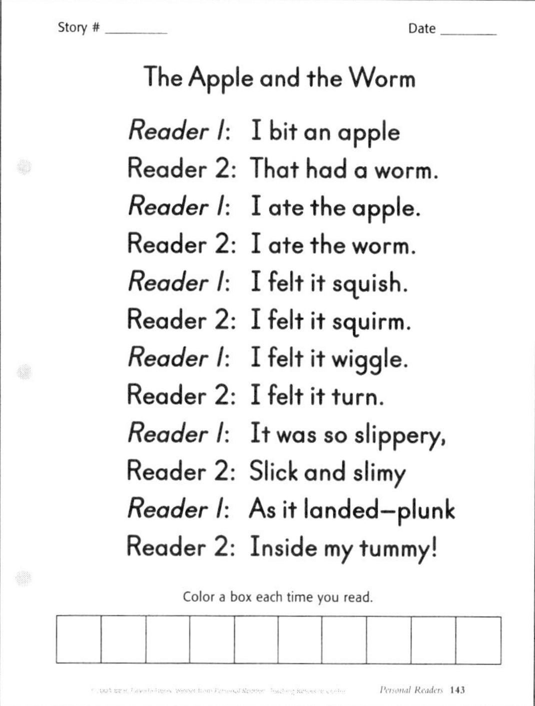
Story # ________ Date ________

The Apple and the Worm

Reader 1: I bit an apple
Reader 2: That had a worm.
Reader 1: I ate the apple.
Reader 2: I ate the worm.
Reader 1: I felt it squish.
Reader 2: I felt it squirm.
Reader 1: I felt it wiggle.
Reader 2: I felt it turn.
Reader 1: It was so slippery,
Reader 2: Slick and slimy
Reader 1: As it landed—plunk
Reader 2: Inside my tummy!

Color a box each time you read.

Personal Readers 143

Story # __________ Date __________

A Worm Riddle

What has rings
But no fingers?
A big, fat worm!

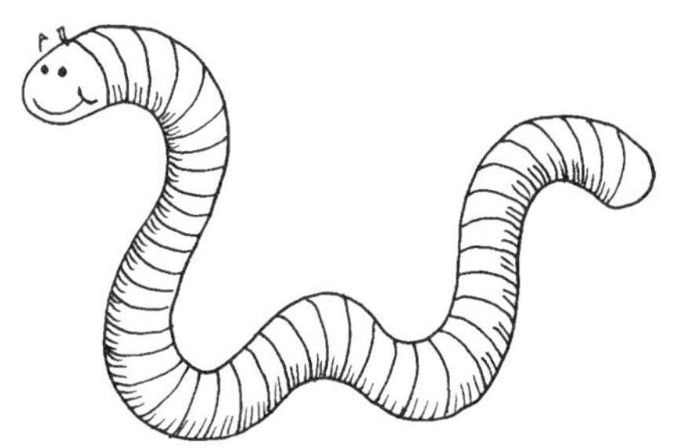

Color a box each time you read.

A Worm Riddle

What has rings

But no fingers?

A big, fat worm!

E	A	R	T	H
W	O	R	M	S
e	a	r	t	h
w	o	r	m	s

Story # __________ Date __________

Nobody Likes Me

Nobody likes me.
Everybody hates me.
Guess I'll go eat worms.

Long, thin, slimy ones
Short, fat, juicy ones
Itsy, bitsy, fuzzy, wuzzy worms

Color a box each time you read.

Nobody Likes Me

Nobody likes me.

Everybody hates me.

Guess I'll go eat worms.

Long, thin, slimy ones

Short, fat, juicy ones

Itsy, bitsy, fuzzy, wuzzy worms

Story # ________ Date ________

The Apple and the Worm

Reader 1: I bit an apple
Reader 2: That had a worm.
Reader 1: I ate the apple.
Reader 2: I ate the worm.
Reader 1: I felt it squish.
Reader 2: I felt it squirm.
Reader 1: I felt it wiggle.
Reader 2: I felt it turn.
Reader 1: It was so slippery,
Reader 2: Slick and slimy
Reader 1: As it landed—plunk
Reader 2: Inside my tummy!

Color a box each time you read.

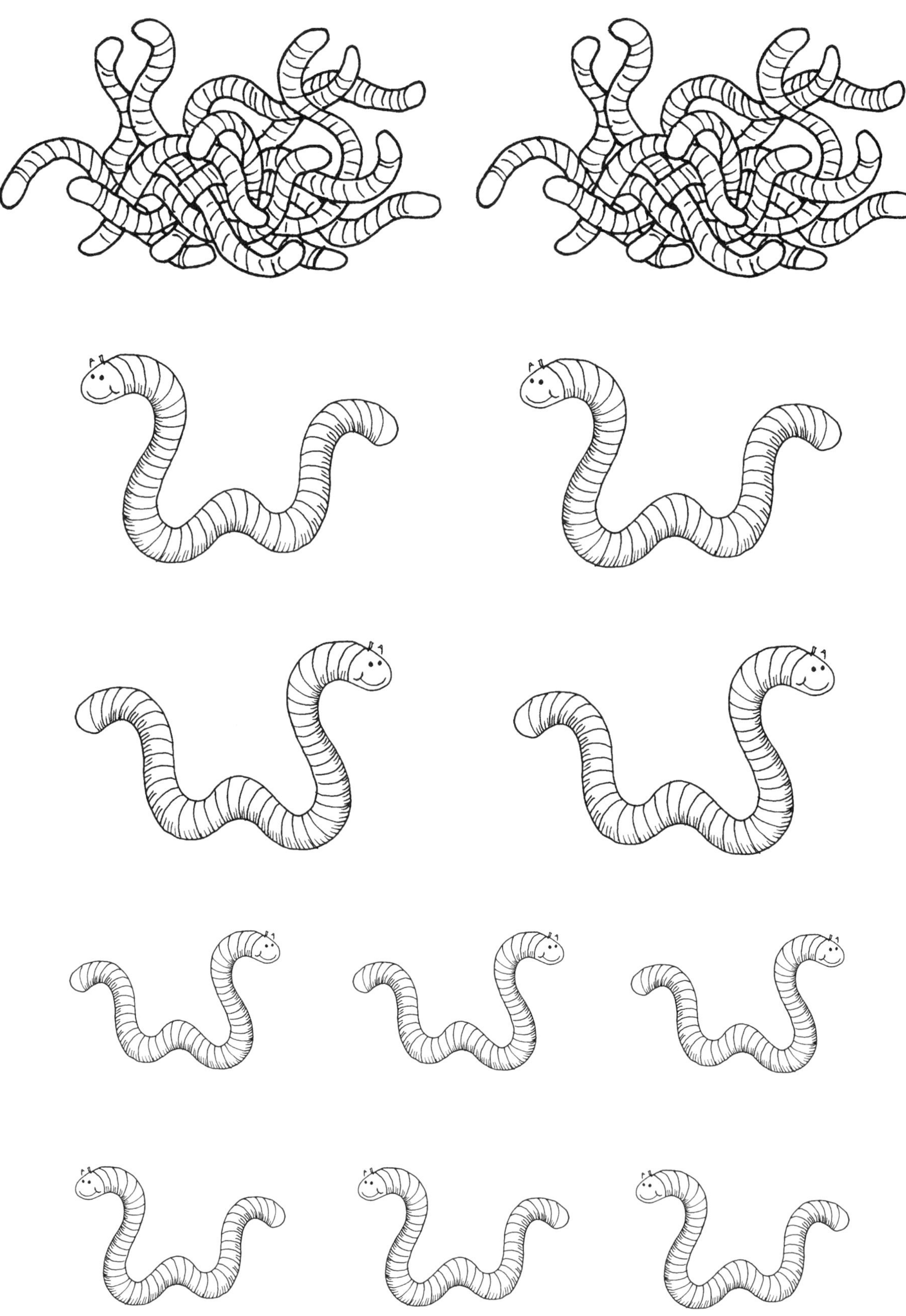

SECTION 3

Management Forms
for Personal Readers

Contents

Parent Note – Emergent Readers 146
Parent Note – Beginning Readers 147
Parent Note in Spanish – Emergent Readers 148
Parent Note in Spanish – Beginning Readers 149
Look What _____ is Reading 150
Personal Reader Reading List 151
Alphabet Graph 152
Letters I Know! 153
Alphabet Award 154
Consonant, Short and Long Vowels Sound Boards 155
Blends and Digraphs Sound Boards 156
Word Bank Word Chips 157
Word Bank List 158
Word Bank Graph: Way to Go! 159
Word Bank Award 160
Word Bank Baseball 161
Bingo Boards Page 164
Boom! Cards Page 165

Dear Parents,

This folder is your child's Personal Reader. In this folder you will find stories that have been created by your child's group and other materials your child has read.

Please have your child read these stories with you and with as many other people as possible. Feel free to have your child read to pets or stuffed animals, too. Have each person your child reads to sign the Personal Reader Reading List or initial the back of the story. This repeated reading helps your child learn to read, learn sight words, and improve reading fluency. Your child will feel like a reader by rereading these materials.

It is very important this folder come back with your child each day!

Here are some other Personal Reader activities:

- Sing the alphabet song while pointing to each letter on the alphabet sticker (on the back of the folder).
- Point to specific letters on the alphabet sticker (no more than 3 to 5) and ask your child to name these letters and/or sounds these letters make.
- Some of the Personal Reader pages will have underlined letters. Ask your child to name them as you point.
- Play games with the letters in the word bank at the back of the reader. Let your child teach you some of the games.
- Tape record your child saying the alphabet or reading one of the stories.

Enjoy these Personal Readers!

Sincerely,

Personal Reader Parent Letter, Emergent Level

Dear Parents,

This folder is your child's Personal Reader. In this folder you will find stories that have been created by your child's group and other materials your child has read.

Please have your child read these stories to you and to as many other people as possible. Feel free to have your child read to pets or stuffed animals, too. Have each person your child reads to sign the Personal Reader Reading List or initial the back of the story. Repeated reading helps your child learn to read, learn sight words, and improve reading fluency. Your child will feel like a reader by rereading these materials.

It is very important this folder come back with your child each day!

Here are some other Personal Reader activities:

- Take turns reading the stories in the Personal Reader.
- Point to specific words in the stories (no more than 3 to 5 per story) and ask your child to read those words.
- Some of the Personal Reader pages will have underlined words in the stories. Point to these underlined words and ask your child to read them.
- Play games with the words in the word bank at the back of the reader. Let your child teach you some of the games.
- Make a copy of the story. Cut the story into lines and let your child put the lines back together.
- Make a copy of a sentence in the story. Cut the sentence into individual words and let your child put the sentence back together.
- Have your child read the list of word bank words quickly.
- Record your child reading one of the stories.

Enjoy these Personal Readers!

Sincerely,

Personal Reader Parent Letter, Beginning Level

Estimados Padres,

Esta carpeta es el Libro Personal de su niño. En esta carpeta se encontrarán los cuentos que han sido creados por su niño y sus compañeros en la escuela. Además, incluye otras materiales que su niño ha leído.

Por favor, dé a su niño oportunidades de leer estos cuentos con usted y con otras personas disponibles. Su niño también puede leer los cuentos a sus animales de casa o juguetes favoritos. Después de que el niño lea, la persona que lo escucha firme la lista de la lectura personal o escriba sus iniciales al final del cuento. Esta lectura repetida ayuda a su niño a leer mejor, a reconocer las palabras de una vista, y a mejorar la fluidez de su lectura. Su niño se sentirá como un lector cuando vuelve a leer estas materiales con más facilidad.

¡Es muy importante que esta carpeta regrese a clase cada día con su niño!

Aquí hay algunas otras actividades que puede hacer su niño con su Libro Personal:

- Canta la canción del alfabeto mientras apunta cada letra en el papel.
- Apunte algunas letras específicas del autoadhesivo del abecedario (no mas de 3 a 5 letras) y haga que su hijo (a) las nombre o diga los sonidos que hacen.
- Hay algunas letras subrayadas en los cuentos. Haga que su hijo (a) las nombre mientras las apunta.
- Participe en juegos con las letras que están en las palabras al fin del Libro Personal. Deje a su niño enseñarle a Vd. algunos de los juegos.
- Grabe una cinta de su niño diciendo el alfabeto o leyendo uno de los cuentos.

¡Esperamos que gocen de estos Libros Personales!

Sinceramente,

Noticias para los padres sobre los Libros Personales, versión emergente (Emergent level)

Estimados Padres,
Esta carpeta es el Libro Personal de su niño. En esta carpeta se encontrarán los cuentos que han sido creados por su niño y sus compañeros en la escuela. Además, incluye otras materiales que su niño ha leído.

Por favor, dé a su niño oportunidades de leer estos cuentos con usted y con otras personas disponibles. Su niño también puede leer los cuentos a sus animales de casa o juguetes favoritos. Después de que el niño lea, la persona que lo escucha firme la lista de la lectura personal o escriba sus iniciales al final del cuento. Esta lectura repetida ayuda a su niño a leer mejor, a reconocer las palabras de una vista, y a mejorar la fluidez de su lectura. Su niño se sentirá como un lector cuando vuelve a leer estas materiales con más facilidad.

¡Es muy importante que esta carpeta regrese a clase cada día con su niño!

Aquí hay algunas otras actividades que puede hacer su niño con su Libro Personal:
- Tomen turnos leyendo los cuentos en el Libro Personal.
- Apunte palabras específicas de los cuentos (no mas de 3 a 5 por cuento) y haga que su hijo (a) lea estas palabras.
- Hay algunas palabras subrayadas en los cuentos. Apúntelas y haga que su hijo (a) las lea.
- Participe en juegos con las palabras que están en la lista de palabras al fin del Libro Personal. Deje a su niño enseñarle a Vd. algunos de los juegos.
- Haga una copia del cuento. Corta el cuento en líneas y deje a su niño poner las líneas en orden bien.
- Haga una copia de una frase en el cuento. Corte la frase en palabras individuales y deje a su niño ponerlas juntas en orden bien.
- Dé a su niño oportunidades de leer rápidamente las palabras en la lista al fin del Libro Personal.
- Grabe una cinta de su niño mientras dice el alfabeto o lee uno de los cuentos.

¡Esperamos que gocen de estos Libros Personales!

Sinceramente,

Noticias para los padres sobre los Libros Personales, versión principiante (Beginning level)

Look what __________ is reading!

Date Started	Title	Number of Rereadings	Date Finished

Personal Reader Reading List

These are selections I have read with my teacher or buddy. They include rhymes, little books, group experience charts, and dictations. Please listen to me read them to you. I am very proud of my reading!

Name: ______________________________

Number in Personal Reader	Title of the Personal Reader Selection	Type: Book, poem, dictation	Tutor/Parent	Date

Alphabet Graph

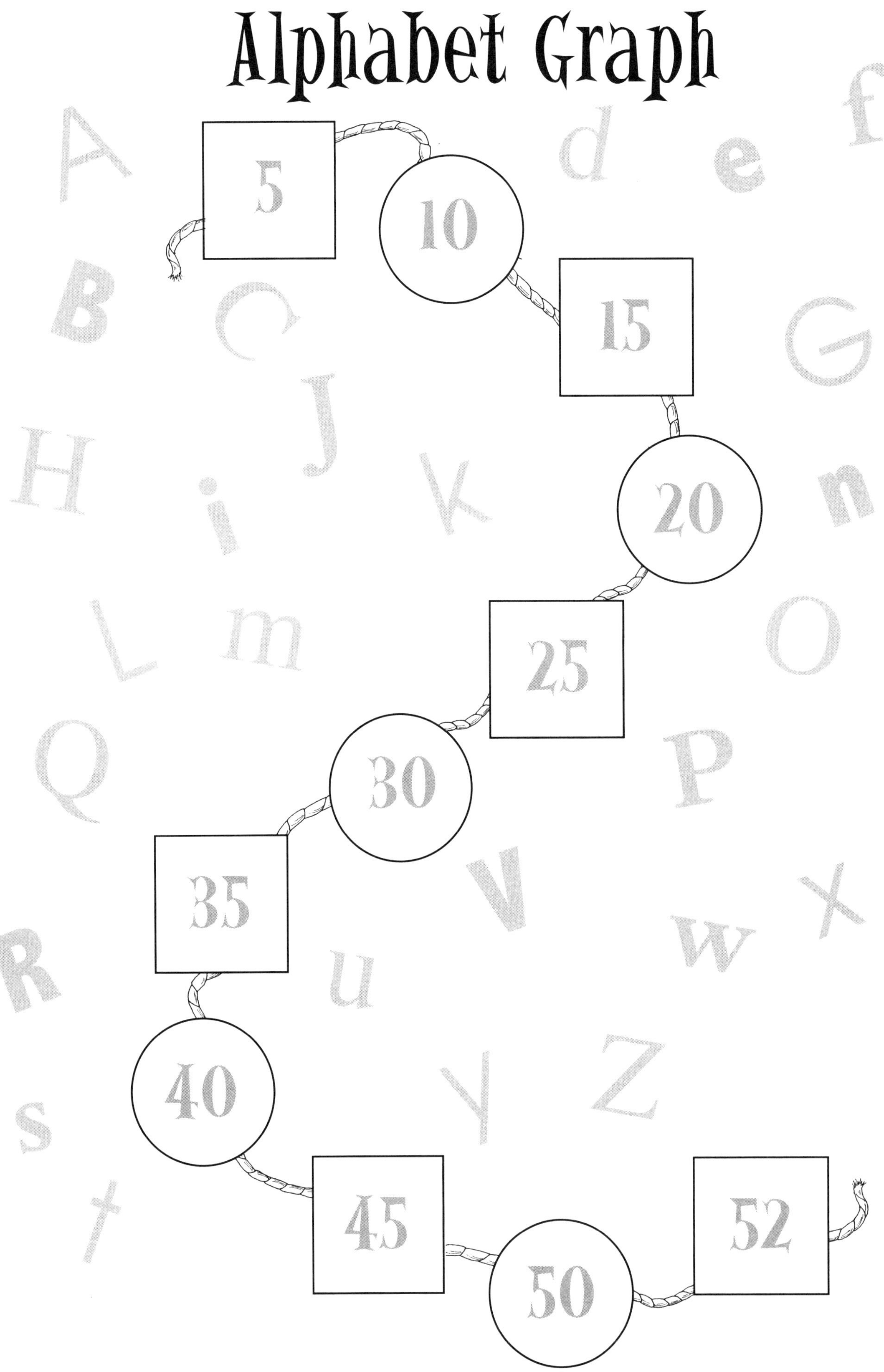

Letters I Know

I am very proud I know the letters that are circled. Point to a circled letter and let me tell you the name, sound, or something that begins with that letter.

Aa	Bb	Cc	Dd
Ee	Ff	Gg	Hh
Ii	Jj	Kk	Ll
Mm	Nn	Oo	Pp
Qq	Rr	Ss	Tt
Uu	Vv	Ww	Xx
Yy	Zz		

Alphabet Award

to

____

for learning _____ letters of the alphabet.

WAY TO GO!!

Teacher ________________________ Date __________

Beginning Consonants	j jump	s sun
b bike	k kite	t tent
c cat	l leaf	v vest
d dog	m mouse	w web
f fish	n nest	y yo-yo
g goat	p pig	z zoo
h house	r ring	#53530640 www.trcabc.com ©2004 Teaching Resource Center

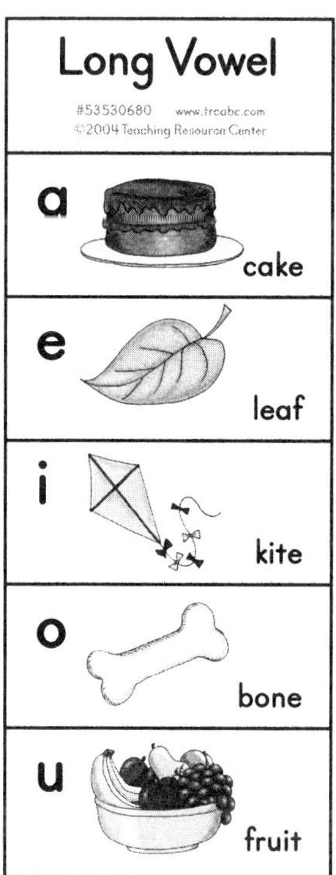

Beginning Blends and Digraphs	br 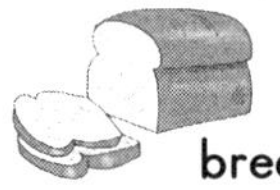 bread	sc  scarf	ch  chair
bl  block	cr  crab	sk  skate	sh  sheep
cl  clock	dr  dress	sm  smile	th  thumb
fl  flag	fr  frog	sn 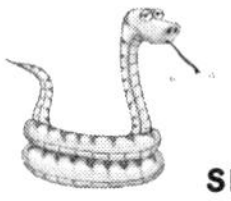 snake	wh  whale
gl 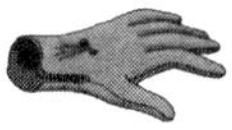 glove	gr  grapes	sp  spoon	qu  queen
pl  plane	pr  pretzel	st  star	tw  twins
sl  slide	tr  train	sw 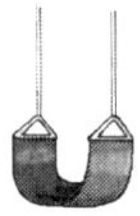 swing	#53530650 www.trcabc.com ©2004 Teaching Resource Center

Word Bank Word Chips

Use this sheet to make word chips for word bank words.
Card stock makes the word chips sturdier.

Word Bank Words for ____________________

These are words I can read. Please initial each time I read them to you. Feel free to make notes on the back of this sheet about how quickly and accurately I read the words.

Word Bank Graph

for

____

WAY TO GO!

Color in a box for every ten words you have in your word bank.

Date: ____	100
Date: ____	90
Date: ____	80
Date: ____	70
Date: ____	60
Date: ____	50
Date: ____	40
Date: ____	30
Date: ____	20
Date: ____	10

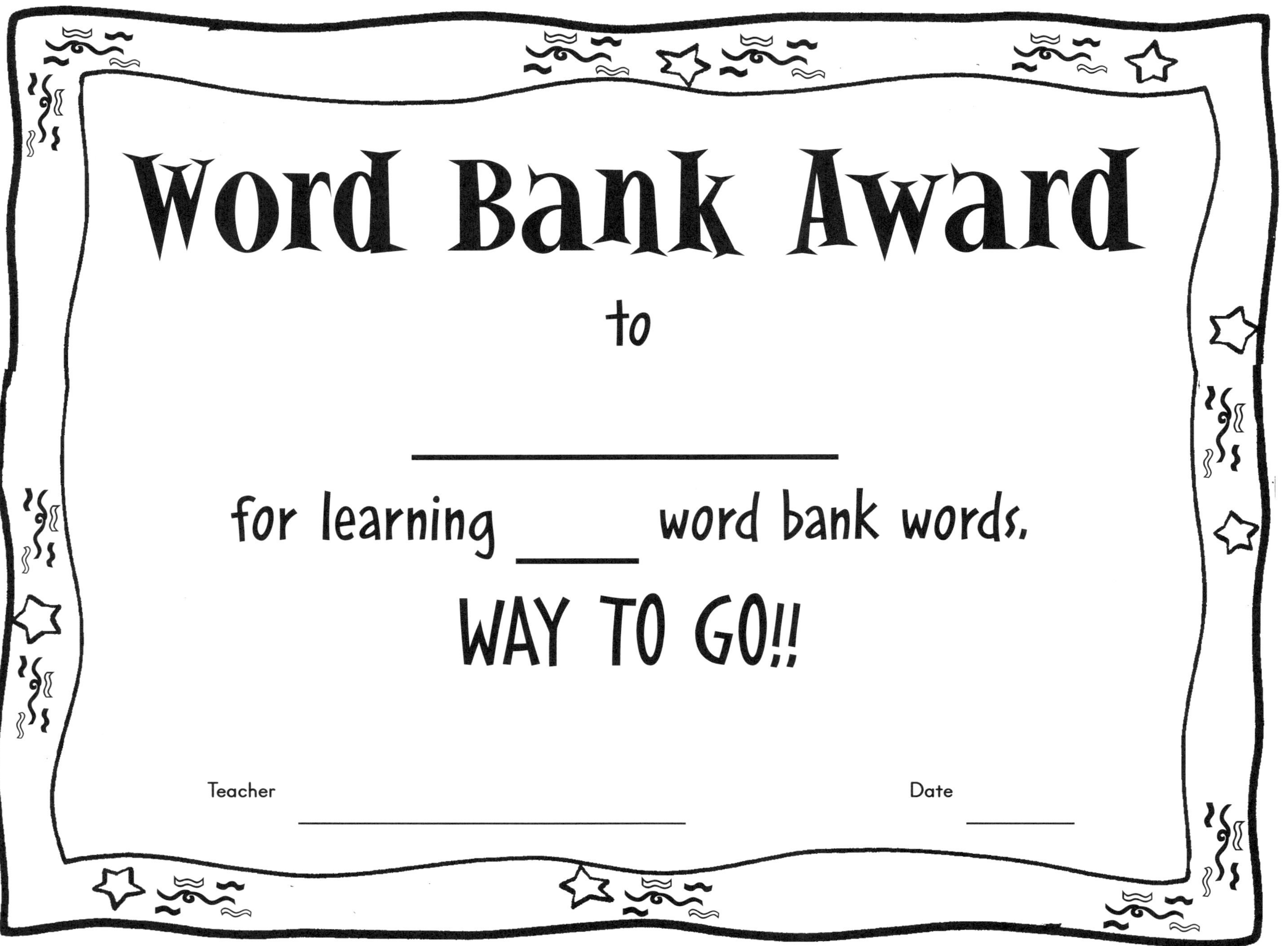
Word Bank Award

to

____

for learning ____ word bank words.

WAY TO GO!!

Teacher ______________ Date ______________

Word Bank Baseball

This game is best played by two people. Each player uses his or her own word bank word chips. Each word chip should have a word the player thinks he or she knows how to read very well. (Students can also use collections of sight words written on word chips for this game).

Materials:

- Word Bank Baseball game board
- Two playing pieces or markers
- Individual word banks or sight words printed on 1" by 3" cards
- Paper on which to record the number of home runs each player makes

Directions

1. Glue the baseball diamond (found on pages 162 and 163) onto the inside of a manila folder.
2. The players write a 1, 2, 3, or 4 on the back of each word chip from their personal word banks.
3. The players mix up the order of their word bank chips.
4. Player 1 puts his marker on home base and places the top five word chips from his pile face-up on the table.
5. Player 1 says one of the words.
6. If it is said correctly, he turns the chip over and moves around the bases according to the number on the back of the chip (i.e., if the number on the back is a 2, then he moves two bases.)
7. If the word is said incorrectly, the player can't move his marker and continues on to the next word.
8. Each time a player passes home base, she earns a run and one point.
9. When player 1 has attempted all five words, the inning is over and he returns to home base until it is her turn again.
10. Player 2 then puts her marker on home and places the top five word chips from her pile face-up on the table and plays her words.
11. The winner is the player with the most home runs when all the words in one player's pile have been used.

Have Fun!

Bingo Board

Boom! Cards

Boom!	Boom!
Boom!	Boom!
Boom!	Boom!
Boom!	Boom!
Boom!	Boom!
Boom!	Boom!
Boom!	Boom!
Boom!	Boom!